TO SAVE
OUR SCHOOLS,
TO SAVE
OUR CHILDREN

TO SAVE
OUR SCHOOLS,
TO SAVE
OUR CHILDREN

The Approaching Crisis In America's Public Schools

by Marshall Frady
The ABC Closeup News Staff
and
Joan S. Dunphy

Judy Crichton,
Richard Gerdau,
Kathy Slobogin,
Joseph Angier,
Thomas Lennon

Introduction by Robert Coles
Foreword by Peter Jennings

NEW HORIZON PRESS
Far Hills, N.J. 07931
Distributed by Scribner's Book Companies, Inc.

Copyright 1985 by New Horizon Press

ABC News segments copyright 1984-1985 American Broadcasting
Co. Inc. Materials Supplied Courtesy of ABC News.

Library of Congress Cataloging-in-Publication Data
Frady, Marshall.
  To save our schools, to save our children.
  Based on the fall 1984 ABC-television program of the same title.
  Bibliography; p.
    1. Public schools——United States——Evaluation.
2. Teachers——United States. 3. Socially handicapped
children——Education——United States. I. Dunphy, Joan S.
II. ABC News. III. To save our schools, to save our
children. IV. Title.
LA217.F64 1985   371'.01'0973   85-18798
ISBN: 0-88282-013-3 (New Horizon Press)
Manufactured in the United States of America

Adapted from

ABC NEWS CLOSEUP

TO SAVE OUR SCHOOLS, TO SAVE OUR CHILDREN

AS BROADCAST OVER THE
ABC TELEVISION NETWORK

TUESDAY, SEPTEMBER 4, 1984
8:00 - 11:00 PM, EST

Students: Produced and Directed by: Richard Gerdau

Teachers: Produced by: Kathy Slobogin
Directed by: Consuelo Gonzalez

Community Faith: Produced by: Judy Crichton
Directed by: Judy Crichton
and Thomas Lennon

Written by: Marshall Frady, Richard Gerdau,
Kathy Slobogin, Judy Crichton
Joseph Angier and
Thomas Lennon

Senior Producer: Richard Richter
Executive Producer: Pamela Hill

With Closeup
Correspondent: Marshall Frady
Host: Peter Jennings

TO OUR CHILDREN

Liberty without learning is always in peril, and learning without liberty is always in vain.

John F. Kennedy

In the interest of readability, the editors have deleted footnotes and complete citations from a number of selections. If the texts are to be used for scholarly/or scientific purposes, it would be well to consult the source notes at the end of the book and obtain a copy of the original text.

Table of Contents

ACKNOWLEDGEMENTS

The material in Parts I, II, III, and IV has been written and edited by the ABC News Closeup staff and adapted from the television documentary "To Save Our Schools, To Save Our Children."

The balance of the book has been authored by Dr. Joan S. Dunphy, with important research and content contributions by Dr. Robert Duke, Dr. Patricia H. Barbaresi, Dr. David Hodesson, Dr. Merrill Skaggs, Dr. Virginia Hyman, Dr. Don LePenta, Dr. Edward Cook, Dr. Scott McDonald, and Ms. Janet Mulvey (who helped draw together and coordinate the multitude of source materials). Dr. Robert Coles honored us with his distinguished introduction. In addition, New Horizon Press gratefully acknowledges research assistance from: Rutgers University, Harvard University, Yale University, Drew University, Long Island University and the University of Miami; plus the numerous schools, associations, corporations, government agencies and private citizens who have responded to our questionnaires, telephone calls and letters. Without these enriching contributions and counselors, this book could not have been completed.

FOREWORD

As the fall semester of 1984 was beginning all across America, schools in the largest of cities to the smallest of hamlets were opening their doors for the new academic year as they had for more than two centuries.

It was at that moment ABC News devoted an entire evening of prime time television to an examination of our system of public education.

"Opening their doors to what?" we asked. And then we proceeded to show and tell more than nineteen million viewers that the nation is facing a grave crisis in the public schools.

The three-hour documentary, "To Save Our Schools, To Save Our Children" opened the doors of the 83,000 public schools to public scrutiny, with the hope of keeping them open for new thinking, planning, and accomplishment.

The program showed us students distracted and handicapped by economics; teachers frustrated and often uninspired; and communities whose educational support is eroding.

The report by correspondent Marshall Frady and the Closeup documentary team was devastatingly on target, often moving and sometimes frightening.

Time will mellow the outrage and dismay triggered by the documentary, but we feel that the real significance of our investigation lies in the future solutions to be found for these feelings and for the crises in our schools which are their real cause.

With this in mind, the decision to adapt the television production into book form has been made. At ABC News we believe that in presenting these ideas in written form where they can be read, reread and evaluated, real progress toward change can be initiated. Those who viewed the original program—the public, educators, politicians and critics—responded with overwhelmingly rave reviews; ABC executives and personnel responsible for "To Save Our Schools, To Save Our Children," were flooded with congratulatory mail and telegrams; educators and political leaders from across the country sent in their responses to our program's producers and directors.

Here is a sampling of the mail that further encouraged and prompted the production of this book:

"I am pleased ABC News committed a significant block of prime time to an issue which is of such great national concern."

Gov. Christopher Bond (Missouri)

"I changed my travel plans so I could watch your TV special. I was glad I did."

Sen. David Boren (Oklahoma)

"It is critical that the American public realize the correlation between education and democracy, that democracy won't survive unless we educate our people."

Sen. Butler Derrick (S. Carolina)

"It was without a doubt the best documentary on education I've seen on television."

Ernest L. Boyer, President
Carnegie Foundation

The New York Times said it was the best network documentary of the year.

The Boston Globe put it well when it said, "This courageous . . . program showed that America, whether in patriotism real or illusionary, old or new, has somehow lost its historic commitment to public education."

The documentary has already won several national honors, including the prestigious Peabody award for excellence. It is this sort of reaction which led us to think that what we found should appear in a more enduring form, and thus the book. We hope that it, combined with the television broadcast, will help stimulate a new spirit of dedication as we all work to change our schools.

No other country has commited so much to public education.

FOREWORD

We have staked the survival of the American dream on an educated citizenry. Our security, our economic competitiveness in the world, our very leadership depends on it.

Peter Jennings
ABC News
New York City
July 1985

INTRODUCTION

In over twenty-five years of work as a pediatrician and child
psychiatrist—work done in various parts of this country, and with
children from a wide range of social, racial and ethnic backgrounds—I have never once talked with a parent who, no matter
the reservations or criticisms expressed when the subject of his
or her child's education was discussed, didn't at some point
mention a strong hope that the country's public schools will
somehow improve. So I have heard even wealthy parents put
it—men and women whose children have always gone to private
schools; and so I have heard the poor say, over and over, as they
try to imagine a life for their sons and daughters that's better than
the present one. Such being the case—a universal yearning for
the improvement of public education in the world's most powerful
nation—one wonders why we must use the word "save" in connection with our schools and our children.

Perhaps I can help the reader, in this regard, by summoning
some witnesses of my own, whose thoughtful and considered
reflections, informally and unselfconsciously spoken in the course
of years of interviews with my wife and me, have many times
given us pause, as Americans, as teachers (she of high school
children, whereas I work in a university) and not least, as the
parents of three sons who have attended schools in both the
northeast and the southwest. Among the most memorable of our
experiences was that of observing school desegregation take place
in the South during the 1960's—black children become pioneers,
and white children learning to change their notions of what is
possible, what is legal and indeed mandatory, so far as the ed-

ucation of black children is concerned. As one black child walked past hostile mobs (in New Orleans) in order to attend school, her mother told my wife this: "It's terrible, what that child has to go through, day after day—but in the long run I can only hope and pray it'll be worth it. We're just poor people, and we don't have one single day of education to our credit, my husband and me. We grew up in a small Mississippi town and our learning consisted of knowing what the white folks expected of you—to go and work their land, plant their crops, and tend them, then harvest them when the right time came. Then the machines came, and slowly, we all had to leave, and we did, and my husband and I, we were glad, because we figured that even if it was hard to live in a big city, and even if we stayed as poor as can be, there'd be one big difference—our kids would go to school and stay in school, and they'd learn and they'd learn, and the result would be that they'd become somebodys, and not be nobodys, like our preacher says we should become.

"That's what we're living for, all of us people who never had much of a chance ourselves—for our children: the hope that they'll have *their* chance. And that has to mean they'll learn to read and they'll learn to write, and they'll find out about everything, so they'll be able to understand the world, and have something to offer it. There isn't a day goes by that I don't ask myself why we're suffering, why we're going through all these troubles—those Klan people shouting at us and telling us they'll kill us; and there isn't a day that I don't tell myself it's worth it, dear Lord, it's worth it, because if you can get an education, I tell my children, then you're on your way, that's what I say to them. When one of them will ask what I mean when I say 'on your way,' then I tell them—on your way to being what God meant us to be, people who can use their heads, and figure things out, and look anyone in the eye and feel their equal. That's what I hear these civil rights people say—and I'll tell you, it's what my grandfather would tell us, and he was the son of a slave: 'Keep hoping you'll get to have schooling,' he'd tell us, 'and if not you, then your children,' he'd always add, and I'll never forget his advice to us, and when my kids became the ones to be the educated ones in our family, then I got down on my knees and thanked almighty God, and remembered my grand-daddy. He told us when he went to bed every night he dreamed that the day would come that one of us kin would be in schools, and would get an education. I think he believed getting an education, going to school—it's the promised land, the place where God will come and show Himself to us! I know it sounds like old grand-daddy was being too hopeful, but he'd given up on everything else, even saying his prayers, he'd say, and so that's all he had, I now realize, those schools he'd dream of for us, who'd come after him!''

Those words are as utterly and concretely and essentially an American statement as one is likely, ever, to encounter—whether in the course of listening to today's Americans or reading about what earlier generations of Americans have had to say. I suppose some of us who are rather more comfortable in background than the above speaker, more assured about ourselves and our families, might well judge ourselves as not likely to be so earnestly sentimental and religiously naive about our children's schooling. Still, lots of quite successful and well-educated people have their own good reasons as parents to wonder about the future, even as that black woman did (not to mention her grandfather), and to do so through reflection on the nature and purpose of education—as was the case, certainly, for a prominent New Orleans lawyer, who also had children of school age in those tumultuous years of desegregation: "I feel sorry for all those people, the white people as well as the Negroes. I know it's fashionable for you Yankees to come down here and bleed for our colored folks, and I'm with you, believe me—even though lots of people in my position would disagree with me, and are just plain mad that we're being put through all this. But just as I watch those mobs on television, those white people screaming and shouting at a little Black girl, I realize that it's not really her they're shouting at. They're bemoaning their own lives, and telling the world that the only chance they've got, to better themselves, to make sure their kids have half a deal out of life—it's through the schools. They probably have been wishing that their kids could have a better education, *apart from this desegregation thing*, and now the racial trouble reminds them of what they've known and felt, and so they run out into the streets and shout—shout their fears and worries.

I suppose I'm 'above' all that, but not really. My son and daughter are only a couple of years older than those kids in that elementary school, and for all the advantages that my wife and I have to offer our children, the first-class private school they attend, and the whole way of living we offer, with private lessons in French and in athletics, and the trips we take—even so, we worry ourselves sick sometimes, when we hear about a teacher we don't like, or when our son, or our daughter, comes home and tells us something that reminds us how fragile any young child can be, and how powerful a school is, *any school*, in the life of a child. A school is the replacement for us—it takes over from us, the parents, and a lot of what our children learn and come to believe is derived from what they've heard and been taught in school.

I know I'm just telling you common sense, what anyone knows. But people think of the troubles these poor folks are having here in New Orleans, and they forget *why* we're having all this trouble, and it isn't only the racial problem: it's the schools—what they mean to every single one of us in the country. Anything that affects the schools gets to our heart and soul, that's how I'd put it. When I see my children leaving for school, even now, I get a little choked up, no matter how lucky they are to be going to a wonderful place, where everything's going well, and they're not lost in some big crowd. We love those two, they're part of us, and we want them to have a truly good day today, and another good day tomorrow, and we know in our hearts that there are lots of things that can go wrong—yes, even in the best school: teachers who say the wrong things and do the wrong things and so your child hears the wrong things and learns the wrong things! And I'm not just talking about formal learning.

INTRODUCTION

I'm talking about everything that goes on—between the children,
and between them and the teacher, and in the halls and out on
the playground as well as when they're eating, or just sitting and
waiting for a class to begin. I have a memory; I remember going
to school, and I remember how my mind was shaped by what
I experienced there. You doctors—you emphasize how important
mothers and fathers are, how important the early years are, before
school starts for the child; but I think a child is tremendously
influenced by school, too. Sometimes I think parents are always
on the defensive trying to stand up for what they believe, because
we lose our young ones to the outside world, no matter how
stubbornly we try to be teachers ourselves! As my wife reminded
me the other day—we see our children less and less; and all we
hear when we're at the supper table is 'at school this,' and 'at
school that.' So, that's what you're seeing on our streets—parents
worried; and don't leave us out, even if we seem to have it made.
We worry, too!

At the time I was more than a little annoyed by those re-
marks—a seemingly possessive (and rivalrous) egoism at work:
his concerns, *his* children—as if he worried that those embattled
white and black parents and children, all so much poorer and
vulnerable than he and his children, might be getting more of
everyone's attention and concern than is their due! But the more
time I spent with him and his family, and with other relatively
privileged families, the more I began to realize that this was,
quite simply, an American parent, one of the millions, no matter
their background, who place enormous emphasis on education,
while at the same time worrying long and hard about what its
purposes are, its over-all significance in the lives of children, and
not least, its effectiveness. As a matter of fact, I have been
surprised (and sometimes stunned) by the outspoken anxieties
and worries I have heard exceedingly well-to-do and influential
parents convey—as they talk about the education of their children.
It is not so much that they are explicitly unhappy with one or
another aspect or a given school. Rather, they are concerned
about the world we live in, the social and cultural changes which

keep pressing upon us, and too, their own ability to make sense of those changes, deal with them as grown-ups, never mind as the mother and father of children. No wonder, then, the schools become major presences, of sorts, in the minds of these (comfortable, successful) people: men and women thoughtful and observant enough to realize that children soon enough pick up a lot of practical and moral knowledge in those classrooms supposedly dedicated purely to academic matters, to the point that an entire (contemporary) world bears down forcefully, indeed—with the parents, often enough, unsuspecting or helpless.

I mention these rather affluent parents, and their children, because sometimes I think discussions and analyses of our schools, and of the problems of American education in general become all too predictably focused on the obvious and deplorable plight of certain schools located in certain communities. We do our poor and vulnerable families no justice if we persist in segregating them this way, never mind in other ways; persist in forgetting that all kinds of parents are dissatisfied with the education of their children in all sorts of ways, and that the sources of such frustration and discontent are, to some extent at least, existential—meaning, connected to the inevitable pangs of apprehension that go with surrendering a child, for all practical purposes, most of the day during most of the year, to the personal and moral authority of others.

Not that (Lord knows) some children don't get put into much worse jeopardy than others do when that school-connected separation from their parents take place. Yet, in this regard, too, I fear we sometimes resort to rather facile stereotypes—the already "difficult" or unpromising or "troubled" ghetto child, say, who is doubly cheated because the school-life available to him or her is as sad and flawed or unnerving or plain destructive as the home-life he or she has known. Again and again my (schoolteacher) wife and I have talked with parents who are having a rough time making a go of things, to be sure, and who obviously have themselves little in the way of intellectually developed resources to offer their children—but who are extremely interested in what the schools offer and might offer, and needless to say, are deeply discouraged about the educational prospects that their particular neighborhood (or even city) offers its young people. These are parents, who, in fact, offer their children a fairly solid home life—only to learn, rather grimly, how little is awaiting their sons and daughters in the schools they attend. We have grown accustomed to the availability among us in America of the tough social critic, the essayist, the muckraking journalist, who relentlessly exposes the various and severe inadequacies of our schools, whether they be the ones in our affluent suburbs or those in our ghettoes. We are less likely by far to know about the ordinary parents, some of them as humble as can be, who possess a shrewd sense of what obtains in this world—men and women who have seen a lot as they have taken their children to school, and have as well had a lot to say.

I now call in witness, for example, a thirty year old "single-parent," a black woman who lives in Boston's Roxbury district, who is on welfare, who is trying to bring up her three children as best she knows how, and who has her own quite precise and knowing observations to make about a particular neighborhood, a particular school system: "We're on the bottom of the ladder, so it's not hard to figure out why our schools aren't so good hereabouts! But I get really mad when I hear on a program someone saying that your welfare mothers aren't trying enough to get jobs, or trying enough to get their kids educated. I take my children to school everyday—walk them. I pray for them to learn and learn. I have them say their prayers, too—that they'll pay attention to the teacher, and remember everything she says, and do what she asks, and be as good as possible, and try to be as smart as the good Lord will let you be. A day doesn't go by, I swear, that I don't tell my children that the school is the one and only hope in their lives—that if we're ever to make something of ourselves, it'll be because we've really, really learned our letters and our numbers.

"I'll tell you something, though: my kids are little, and they do listen to me, still—but I can tell that they're not convinced when they hear me talk about school. They go there, and I guess they know! I try to tell them what they should believe. I hold up the Bible to them, and say prayers for them, and they hear me, and I keep my chin up, and I hope they'll keep their chins up. When they're in that [school] building, though, I know it's different. I've been inside. I've seen the mess there, the noise and the rooms so crowded lots of kids don't have desks, and each day, I hear, there's a new [substitute] teacher, and it's not a place a kid believes will help him out, because he knows he's got to fight all day in school just to hold on to his belongings, because there's all that fighting and stealing, and the teachers don't care; they've given up, and they're putting in their time to collect their money each day, and my kids know that, and no wonder they give me a funny look when I talk about how important school is!''

For years I've heard parents come to this crucial realization—the distinction between their educational ideals, as they are constantly spoken to their children, and the tough, harsh realities of this life, so hard for young people to comprehend. As the reader goes through this book, some of it an exceedingly unsettling reminder to America of the serious handicaps, impasses, and obstacles so many of our children face with respect to their education, I hope this woman's continuing moral struggle will not be forgotten. Like millions of other parents, she wants the very best for her children—sees in their future the main meaning of her own life. Like millions of other parents, she exhorts her children, holds up to them ideals and aspirations, hopes and promises—an effort to tame the potential wildness all of us have, an effort to inspire ambition and confidence and determination. Yet, her children know otherwise, already—even at eight or nine years of age; know the hustle and horror of a terribly over-crowded, under-staffed school, where facilities are inadequate, where teachers are exhausted or all too fearful or sad or cynical or frustrated.

For a long time many of us have worried about the children who attend such classrooms—their ''motivation'' (or the lack of it), their background, their psychological and intellectual resources (or again, the lack of them). But our concerns have been

INTRODUCTION

no larger, I think it fair to say, than those of the woman just quoted—than those of millions of American mothers and fathers, who are very involved in their children's educational life, who try hard to teach them how to be decent and conscientious individuals, and who look to the schools as necessary allies in that endeavor, only to realize, all too soon, that such is not necessarily the case. The issue is, then, not the absent aspirations of parents, or the devilish inertia or unruliness of children; the issue is the everyday reality which both parents and children, not to mention teachers, have to face in countless school districts across the land—the awful and disheartening disparity between what might be and what is, all too exactly noticed and understood by our children, whom we keep calling our future, yet treat as if we care not what that future might be, ought to be.

Robert S. Coles
Cambridge, Massachusetts
1985

TO SAVE
OUR SCHOOLS,
TO SAVE
OUR CHILDREN

PART I

The Perilous Decade:
STUDENTS

It is at once the most commonplace of happenings and, still, the most astonishing, its individual mystery undiminished by immemorial million-fold repetitions: a human birth—and suddenly, out of nothingness, a mind begins. A mind that holds possibilities for knowing—for wonder, for curiosity—as wide as the universe.

From this first instant of measureless possibility, that mind commences a journey toward its potential, second, larger birth: toward knowledge. A journey toward light—or blindness. Toward possessing its world and the accumulated heritage of its time, or becoming captive and victim of it.

That mind, that potential, is finally the subject of all that follows here. And on the progress of the journey of that mind and of millions like it—on something so tenuous and complex and impalpable—hangs nothing less, ultimately, than the strength or decline of this nation.

That long, uncertain odyssey toward understanding will largely take place, and its outcome decided, in America's public schools. But our vast system of public education is now approaching a crisis deeper than any it's faced before.

A few months before his retirement late in 1984, U.S. Secretary of Education Terrell Bell observed: "Human intelligence is the prime resource in this country. It's not the natural resource anymore that counts—it's human intelligence. And we're faced with competitors—intelligent, highly motivated competitors—in other nations. And we're one global village. Maybe our time has passed,

3

as has happened in other civilizations. And whether we can renew ourselves and regain our vigor as a nation, I think largely depends on how well we educate our people.''

Once again for America's young, as summer's last bright nights of windy freedom wheel to an end, there returns a long and familiar national rite across the broad reaches of the land. With premonitions already in the air of the cool smokes of autumn, some forty million of our children begin to pass back through the doors of America's public schools—an institution, an idea, as old as this democracy.

No other nation has, for so long, committed to public education so much of its hopes, meaning, its energy, as has the United States. Virtually since Jefferson, a system of public schools has been one of America's fundamental articles of faith. With our widely varied assembly of people, they were really to be the common schools for democracy. The vitality and survival of the American Ideal—and, indeed, our security, our eminence, our economic leadership, among the nations of the world—we have staked on an educated, enlightened citizenry.

That dependency endures. 89 percent of America's elementary and high school students are now in public schools across this land. Nearly three-quarters of those children are white, mostly descendents of our original and now largely assimilated immigrants—the Irish, the Germans, Italians, Jews, Poles. Sixteen percent of this vast public school population is black. Another 10 percent now is Hispanic and Asian, among the children of the newest tides of immigration from Central America, the Caribbean, from Southeast Asia.

1. The Alarm Now

But in this autumn of 1985, as America's children are returning to our system of public schools, that fundamental national institution is itself poised on the threshold of a decade of peril—a precarious moment of truth which could decide the survival or final decay of our whole concept of public schooling.

4

Not since the shock of Sputnik in 1957, when Soviet science lifted a satellite into space far ahead of us, has there stirred a wider unease about the state of America's schools. And the sense of crisis, this time, has not come from shocks without, but from discoveries of decay within.

Over the years, we have passed through recurrent alarms about the state of our schools. But the crisis we are now approaching is far deeper and more complex. The most obvious distress signals we've noticed: sinking test scores over the nation, increasingly overloaded and underfunded schools, drift and confusion over actual goals and purposes, and unsettling signs of a tendency toward a separation into two unequal class divisions within the public school system itself.

Underlying these clear alarms are less obvious, more fundamental, compounding threats over the next decade: a growing population of alienated, indifferent, disconnected students; the emergence of a new and different student majority, increasingly from broken families, increasingly non-white, poorer, more culturally impoverished; a generation of fewer and less fit teachers to cope with these more difficult students; a mounting majority of childless or aging Americans with no direct interest in the fate of the public schools at all; a widening disaffection with public school among community tax payers in general, portending a progressive abandonment by those who hve principally carried the system in the past.

Among the most immediate alerts were recent tests and surveys indicating a national depression in learning:

- —SAT scores in 1980 plunged to an all-time low, and while starting to recover, they continue to falter well below the scores of the 1960s.
- —Thirteen percent of the nation's high school graduates read and write at a sixth grade level.
- —Twenty-three million of our adult population have been found to be functionally illiterate.
- —Only half of the seventeen-year-olds in one national survey

5

could compute what percentage thirty is of sixty.

—The drop-out rate of our high school youth is 25 percent nationally, 35 percent in Georgia, and 50 percent in some inner-city environments.

—In public four-year colleges, remedial math courses had to be increased 72 percent between 1975 and 1980.

—Matched against other industrialized nations, American students placed last in seven out of nineteen academic tests—and first in none of them.

—And even among our best students, the number of those scoring over 650 on the verbal part of the Scholastic Aptitude Test plunged 45 percent between 1972 and 1982.

Several of those stunning statistics were cited in the 1983 National Commission Report, "A Nation at Risk", which offered this sobering conclusion: "If an unfriendly foreign power had attempted to impose on America the mediocre educational performance that exists today, we might well have viewed it as an act of war."

The battery of grim statistics speaks not only of dying hopes and possibilities for millions of individual students. It has raised a growing concern now about a national danger—that the next generation of Americans will be far less fit to compete in the world's increasingly sophisticated technological economy. Instead, we may be left with a "lost generation" of students—only vaguely literate, barely competent, adrift in a relentlessly more demanding world—and that would indeed leave us all, in the words of the national commission report, "a nation at risk."

In particular, it's the vast middle majority of our students who have shown the most precipitous slide in learning—precisely that majority on whom America's prospects finally rest for the difficult business of sustaining our democracy, and maintaining our strength and security, through the complex and rigorous challenges of the next century.

In dismay over all this, many of us have been tempted to look for answers in the classroom of what seems a steadier, surer past—in the mirages of nostalgia.

I remember the way it was, for instance, along the dimly gleaming mellow corridors, fragrant of pencil dust and apples and old varnish, at Joseph R. Lamar in Augusta, Georgia, where I began school—in Mrs. Busbee's fifth-grade glass, struggled with the multiplication tables; discovered, in Mrs. Hill's classroom, the geographies of the greater unseen globe beyond that musing little river town; in Miss Bostick's class, awoke into yet another wider world, the great life of literature, Hawthorne, Tennyson, Dickens. And every schoolday was tidily ordered, beginning with The Lord's Prayer and the pledge to the flag—all presided over by Principal McCollum's brisk disciplinary paddle.

Now, many of us would like to think that all it would take to set right *our* children's schools would be that simple discipline, piety, the *rudiments* again—an illusion which our president himself, Ronald Reagan, has politically invoked.

But consider: when many of us were in school in the Fifties, it was a time before computers, really before the great atmospheric impact of television, before our great reaching into space. The community around Joseph R. Lamar Elementary School then, like much of American society, was snugly segregated. America was still at its unchallenged high noon of power and pride in the world. We seemed to know who we were—our values secured by secure families, secure communities, a secure faith in our churches.

How all of that—that America, that world—has since profoundly changed, describes the profound new challenges now confronting our schools; challenges far more expansive and elaborate than any answers to be found in the classrooms of our past.

It's true that since the release of the *Nation at Risk* report, there have been tentative signs of some modest recovery in our public school system—for instance, a small rise in SAT scores during 1984. But the real danger is that our schools still face a decade of gathering crisis wider in magnitude than ever before, one really different in kind.

It is different, ironically, because it is made up of the converging ramifications precisely of our democratic ambition for our schools.

7

CHAPTER I

Over the last few decades, America's schools have been pressed into a staggering social and egalitarian mission of a scale and complexity undertaken by no other nation on earth.

First of all, we've mandated our schools to educate virtually *all* the children of this hugely variegated society—black and white, rich and poor, gifted and handicapped—and to educate them through high school, educate them finely and excellently with equal opportunity for each to realize their full potential and needs. One indication of this awesomely widened reach is that, in 1950, only half our school age population were graduated from high school, while today we've enlarged it to 72 percent.

"We're trying to do something," declares Albert Shanker, President of the American Federation of Teachers, "that no other country in the history of civilization has ever tried to do. We're trying to educate every single child in the country."

"It's a relatively new aspiration to educate children through the twelfth grade," says Dr. Diane Ravitch, Professor of History at the Teachers College of New York. "It's something of a phenomenon in the history of the world. It's part of the American Dream to educate everyone and to educate them very well. No nation has had the historic commitment that we have had to educate all people to their fullest capacity. That's why we're so critical of our schools today."

At the same time, that dramtically amplified *academic mandate has been accompanied by an equally amplified social* mandate.

As the institutions of family and church have weakened in American life, expectations have devolved on our schools to take up the slack—to compensate for the waning of traditional values and the dissolution of the family with special services and counseling and even courses with titles like "American Values" and "Social Behavior." In fact, many analysts see the public school succeeding the home, the church, the community, as the central social institution in American life.

Also, we have asked our public schools to achieve what all the rest of us, all the engines of government and housing laws and popular will, have so far failed or declined to do: to close the old

8

implacable divides of race and class in this country, and at last accomplish one, integrated, true American community. This effort could be considered the second, great Jeffersonian democratic mission consigned to America's public schools.

All of this we've asked our schools to do, with all our children, all at once. Some of the consequences can be glimpsed at one high school in Silver Spring, Maryland—Montgomery Blair.

Set among the calm wide lawns of a leafy suburban neighborhood, a sprawling building with that familiar, geometrically-stenciled glass-and-pastel look of schools built in the Fifties, Montgomery Blair holds an image of the enormously expanded task that has fallen on public schools—and of their uncertain future. Up until a decade or so ago, almost all Blair's students were white, from middle-class homes and a comfortably common world. Now, it labors to serve a chaotic variety of students who seem collectively to mirror all the dislocations and flux of the national community itself. Contained within its clamoring halls and classrooms are children of the desperately poor as well as of the middle class, children from shattered families, students ranging from the brightest to the slowest, and children speaking, in all, twenty different languages. Blair's population is now 63 percent minority, including the children of the newest surges of immigration to this country, from Southeast Asia, from Latin America. "Stick a pin in every trouble spot on the globe," says Blair's earnest, young, vest-suited principal, Joseph Villani, "and you'll have a picture of where our students come from."

Among them is a class of Vietnamese youths, many of whom filtered eventually to this suburban American school from the exodus of the boat people, some of them having witnessed their parents killed by pirates. To watch them now intently straining their way into the language of this new land of theirs—and to watch the effort, in this American classroom, to bring these latest castoffs and waifs of history also into the main life and promise of this country—is stirring to behold. Schools like Montgomery Blair are, in a sense, like the new Ellis Islands, the windows of entry into citizenship in this nation's conglomerate family of peoples—and

9

where there is found forming the new face of America.

But the hugely widened commission of public schools like Blair has brought back into urgent focus a long and still-unresolved question of public education: exactly what should all these children be taught, and to what ends? Just what, after all, should education do? What's it for? To train our young to function and relate in society? To protect the strength of the nation? Or—perhaps more largely, and most authentically serving those other ends—to awaken a child to his wider world, to his wider past, to a memory reaching far beyond his birth: in short, to civilize? That question has become vastly more complicated with the magnified burden on public schools, producing a fitful and kaleidoscopic profusion of courses—again, as can be glimpsed at Blair.

In one classroom, social studies are being taught in Spanish. Down the hall, a collection of students speaking a farrago of different languages is grappling with elementary English readers. Nearby, an all-black class makes its way through a lesson in Black History. Elsewhere, seniors are listening to a lecture on "personal growth" and the changing American family. Outside by the gym, students in vocational education huddle around a car learning how to repair its engine. Upstairs in an advanced English class, seniors are comparing poems by William Carlos Williams and T. S. Eliot for their intimations of death in the sweet quickenings of spring-time. Another class is laboring through remedial math and science, while the school nurse is lecturing a group of pregnant teenage girls on child care.

Not surprisingly, the dizzying spectrum of new responsibilities assigned to our schools has produced deep misgivings among many parents. Can such an egalitarian mass ambition be reconciled with assurances of quality? Can public schools, with so wide a mission, also educate well? The concern, as Dr. Diane Ravitch puts it, is that schools "are so overburdened with responsibilities of many kinds, that somehow their basic responsibility for education has been overwhelmed by all of these other needs."

At Montgomery Blair, it is a hectic battle to nurture its disparate array of students into at least serviceably knowledgeable and com-

petent citizens. "I wouldn't pretend to say we provide quality to everyone," admits Villani. "What we provide is the level of instruction that the student needs—and for some students, that level is at excellence level, for other students, it's at survival level. When people are starting very far behind, the most we can hope to do is to get them up to speed. They may not win the race—but they'll be running."

All the while, Blair must constantly struggle to keep uneasy middle class parents from withdrawing their children, and to keep its harried teachers in its classrooms. "I don't know that we're not getting near the breaking point," Villani acknowledges.

Yet in its distracted but game battle to answer the democratic task imposed on it, Montgomery Blair—like so many similar public schools now across the nation—holds a peculiar energy and exhilaration. "You get an extra knowledge," declares a girl from the advanced English class. "I wouldn't want to give it up for a private school with cliques." And what would be lost, a group of other Blair students were asked, if the effort undertaken by public schools like Montgomery Blair were lost? "Diversity," they chorused, "Life! . . . Everybody'd be the same. Little clones."

Principal Villani offers, "The upper middle class will take care of its sons and daughters through private schooling, as was done a long time ago. But I don't believe that's what the American ideal is all about. What is at stake is the future of a heterogeneous America, an America which provides equal opportunity for everyone, not just for those who can afford to pay. . . . There is something beneficial to learning what the world is all about, that we are no longer Northern European and no longer white, blond-haired folk. This is a country of multiple cultures, and they show up here, and people learn to deal with that. And learn there is a richness there."

But the grand democratic endeavor recently taken on by our public schools has also become the source of many of their tribulations now. Embracing so many more students and ambitions, they have become entangled in a new complex of fundamental, compounding threats:

11

CHAPTER I

—Seismic changes in the ways Americans live and work are leaving a growing population of disconnected, alienated students. Among them are "latch-key" children, youngsters left alone at home by divorced or working parents, without the structured support and care so essential in the early years. Meanwhile, the children of poverty with their own desperate learning problems are spilling into our schools in mounting numbers. Finally, by the time many students reach high school they have become detached, assimilated into this society's pop-electronic culture, a kind of academically autistic world of simple flash and sound and quickness, estranged from all the measured processes of learning and understanding. "This is a different generation," says a high school teacher in California "that places education at the lowest priority." And Dr. Diane Ravitch observes, "There is the lure of that world of television, drugs, the street life, the adolescent culture, the dissolution of the family. Teaching is harder than it ever was."

—Struggling to cope with these divergent students is a national corps of teachers increasingly beleaguered by multiplying duties, oppressive conditions, meager pay, and a disdain by society. A once-revered profession is now caught in a troubling pattern of decline, its ranks diminishing, drifting toward mediocrity. "It's been a decaying profession," says Dr. John Goodlad, Professor of Education at UCLA, "in that the income for teachers has declined against every other occupation in our society except housecleaning."

—Finally, there is the elemental threat, with schools so embattled, of a loss of faith by the American people themselves. There is emerging in this country a majority of childless or aging citizens with no direct personal interest at all in the fate of public schools. And all the disarray of the recent past—looser discipline in the vertigoes of the Sixties, sinking test scores, the turbulence over desegregation—has produced a general disaffection with public

12

schools among community tax payers, especially those in our great metropolitan centers, portending a final abandonment by the middle-class citizens who have principally supported those schools in the past. Already, with dwindling resources, inner-city school systems are becoming educational ghettoes, struggling to contend with a swelling population of students from poor, disadvantaged homes.

Today, large regions of America have more predominantly segregated schools than a decade ago. Despite scattered, impressive successes—most conspicuously, perhaps, in the South— much of the nation at large seems to be receding into a pervasive new pattern of segregation—a situation especially pronounced in the case of Hispanics. The grand endeavor to integrate those schools has produced a backfire unexpectedly wide and treacherous. Confrontations over busing and court-ordered integration plans did not so much resolve the problem as reshape it.

Whites—some unwilling to relinquish deep-seated racial animosities, others not wanting their children to be handicapped by the learning problems of minorities who had suffered generations of oppression, ignorance and neglect—simply abandoned many of the schools being forced to integrate. They fled the cities in such great numbers that—over time—the new pattern of resegregation emerged. Today, Blacks, Hispanics, the poorer, more culturally impoverished children dominate 23 of the nation's 25 largest school systems. White dominance of the richer, suburban schools ringing the cities raises the spectre of a permanent, two-class system. Poor and minority test scores still remain firmly at the bottom of the scale, and reinforce the division. Changing demographic trends in the next decade threaten to make the split irrevocable.

These sociological factors have raised the spectre of a permanent fissure of our urban schools into two separate and dangerously unequal class systems—one, on the fringe of our cities, privileged, affluent, mostly white; the other, in our cities' centers, poorer, mostly minority, wastelands of mediocrity at best, at worst warehouses for the young of the destitute and unhoping, the children of the nether-regions of American society.

Such a dichotomy in our schools would not only effectively abort, for millions of our children, the American promise, but in the end would act to lock the nation itself into a combustibly class-divided society by institutionalizing that division in our schools, so imperiling our very democratic life and thereby tragically reversing the very ideal of public education.

That potential tragedy is a prospect now being fought in Kansas City, Missouri, where one mother, Sue Fulson, who is white and a member of the district board of education, warns, "What happens to these kinds if we refuse to educate them for twelve years through the system—when they get grown up, and they look around, they can't be anything they want, they can't even get a job?"

Dr. Theodore Sizer, Chairman of the Education Department at Brown University, declares, "Somehow, the American people have to act on what they assert, which is we all benefit from the proper education of everybody's youngster. We say it, but we don't act on it."

In the end, though, what we are dealing with is not simply national interests, or curricular, or belabored teachers, or bond issues. In looking at all that, we're really dealing with something much more personal—more intangible and elusive, but vital, intimate, precious: what's happening to the minds of our children in the public schools to which we have entrusted them? *Their* lives, their futures in our communities and in this country—that is what this story is ultimately about.

To tell that story, we will look at several communities and school systems across the country: the Maryland suburb of Silver Spring, where Montgomery Blair High School is located; the city of Los Angeles; the state of Arkansas; and Kansas City, Missouri. The stories of the children in those places—what they're learning, what they're losing—and of their teachers, their families, and the different social conditions surrounding them—are particular reflections of the impending crisis facing our nation over the next decade.

14

The truth is, however, we have not one monolithic national school system, but thousands of separate and independent local ones. This means that, unlike so many other formidable concerns today about our future—the arms race, the contamination of our environment—which seem hopelessly beyond our individual influence, the danger to our schools is the one great issue that *is* within our reach, our hands to personally affect and decide. It is a matter as close and immediate as our own neighborhoods, our own communities—indeed, as our own children.

2. The Children of the Dispossessed

The children. Beyond everything else, they are finally what our impending crisis is about.

Yet, the most intractable and confounding difficulty confronting our schools over the next decade is the different nature of the students they will be expected to teach. Radical changes in American culture are shaping a generation of students who are less disciplined than before, less motivated, in numerous ways more separated from the classroom. And generational cycles of poverty in this country is casting a forbidding burden on our schools.

But if these children fail, if they are not salvaged—we all fail, whether we have the children in school or not.

In the old center of Kansas City, Missouri, are the quarters of its poor—neighborhoods that have, rather than the looming Dostoyevskian grimness of the ghettoes of New York or Chicago, a flat trivial cluttered drabness familiar to most communities across the nation as their own streets of the lost and despairing: slumped vacant buildings, shabby lots, derelict cars, an eternal scatter of miscellaneous refuse among which a human tumbleweed of the defeated and discarded drift and wander through a blank repetition of meaningless days. This is the world from which many of Kansas City's school children come—a world waiting to claim them, too.

Up to a third of the children entering kindergarten in Kansas City, Missouri, are found to be already educationally at risk, true casualties of poverty before they've even begun school. In deep

15

alarm over this, Kansas City in 1980 began testing pre-schoolers expressly to identify those with early learning handicaps. Other recent studies have duplicated the results of the Kansas City study, and have discovered that reading liabilities for the children of the poor can begin as early as two-and-a-half.

Growing numbers of these culturally deprived children are now collecting in our schools. "The social problems are being created at such a rate, it's going to be very difficult for schools to catch up," says Dr. James Comer, child psychiatrist at Yale Medical School. "Many have not had the kind of family experience which would allow them to grow and have the ability to think, plan, organize, the kind of discipline, the kind of ability to sit still and concentrate. . . . And if they don't get it, their chances of being successful economically, as family members, as citizens is very small. They're on a downhill course from kindergarten forward."

Dr. Goodlad submits, "Coping with this is going to be a necessity, and it makes the educational job much tougher than it used to be, and it makes recommendations that ignore this unrealistic."

The children of poverty—especially, in our cities, minority children—remain prisoners of a long and brutalizing legacy of racism and economic exile. Repeating generations of unemployment, welfare, dead-end futility, have worked to shatter the family structure, leaving many youngsters without the role focus of fathers, and with mothers so overwhelmed by pressures, they are unable to provide discipline and order in their children's lives. Those families, largely but not all minority, have been trapped in America's urban ghettoes and pockets of rural poverty so long, that they have lost real connection to the work ethic, lost most sense of structure, lost faith in schools as a means out of the ghetto and up the economic ladder, lost any hope or vision that they might have transferred to their children to help them escape through schooling. Caught in this social undertow, the learning difficulties such children bring to school are desperate. From homes usually barren of books, of any vocabulary of ideas, they enter school already lagging behind and, year after year, fall yet further behind. Large numbers of them from the very start of their school career, face an overwhelmingly uphill struggle—a struggle which a few will win, many will lose, and others will simply give up on. And as more disadvantaged children come into the school system over the next decade, the problem will be overwhelming.

Disadvantaged children of all races, according to the Census Bureau, are being born at a rate significantly higher than that of children from families above the poverty line. Beyond that, authorities warn that the rising numbers of children now being born to teenage and unwed mothers will confront the schools with yet more children deprived of stable home structures, with language and even health deficiencies.

Surely, the profoundly difficult problems of underclass students have troubled schools for decades. What is different now is that underclass problems appear to be intensifying—with no change in sight. The latest figures show that some 53 percent of all black children are born out of wedlock. The average age at which black mothers give birth to their first child is now sixteen-and-a-half. And most disquietingly, as underclass students come into public schools, black and white middle class parents are increasingly tempted to remove their children from the chaotic public education provided in our cities.

Yet the need to assimilate minorities into our schools is expanding rather than diminishing. It is predicted that within a decade, for example, two-thirds of the school-age population in California will be made up of minority students. Clearly—if the democratic ideal of equal education for everyone is to survive—change must come not only from within the schools themselves, but also from within the communities which so desperately depend on them.

The odds hanging over the future of disadvantaged children are forbidding. How poverty tends to reproduce itself was indicated in one recent Department of Education study, which found a striking correlation between poverty and learning disabilities: children from homes with yearly incomes below five-thousand dollars tested at only *half* the level of children from homes with incomes over twenty-one thousand.

At the end of the school day, Kansas City's inner-city children return to the world of the perpetually poor, a world that wars against all the calm and ordered processes of learning—glum and disheveled neighborhoods of turmoil, clamor, tension, flashes of violence.

Chauncy Coody is one of those children. A quiet, grave, watchful black youngster, as a second-grader he came home to a top-floor apartment in a bleak brick barracks-like building climbing sagging sullen stairs clangoring with radios and television sets from other apartments. With his mother on welfare and looking for work, Chauncy was often shuttled among relatives and neighbors until his mother returned. "If she's not home by six or seven o'clock," said Chauncy in a subdued, husking voice, "we just go up to my grandmother's, the manager's, or just come in the house and wait for her to get home. . . . It's a little lonely," he adds. "Sometimes I have to lock up by myself."

Asked if his father were around, Chauncy said simply, "No." How often does he see him? "Every . . . once a month. Because he lives out of town." But Chauncy's mother, a thin young intense woman with snapping black eyes, admitted that Chauncy saw his father, at most, only three times a year. "He misses him a lot, you know. He hates the fact that his father and I aren't together."

Not only is Chauncy's home life unsettled, but the neighborhood surrounding him is one of constantly impending violence. "I do check our windows, 'cause, like when they're fighting, they sometimes use guns and stuff, and I just don't want to get hurt."

"You hear occasional shots," said Chauncy's mother, "but I really never pay any attention. . . . You don't, you know, you don't see the police."

Disadvantaged children like Chauncy enter school not only without the sense of stability so crucial to learning, but with a grimly different vision of the world. "You have to let them know," says Chauncy's mother, "at an early age, that the world is cruel. You know, that the world is cruel."

"It's like a jungle sometimes, it makes me wonder how I keep from going under.

Broken glass everywhere. . . Rats in the front room, roaches
in the back. Junkies in the alley with the baseball bat.
I tried to get away, but I couldn't get far, 'cause a man
repossessed my car.
Don't push me, 'cause I'm close to the edge. I'm trying not to
lose my head . . . Grand Master Flash and The Furious Five
"The Message"

Dr. James Coleman defines the major educational problems of
the underclass as "the absence of consistency, the absence of
structure and the total absence of verbal skills." Those crippling
academic deficits coincide with social cripplings. Schools are
asked to introduce authority and disciplining to children who have
no authority and discipline, to children who operate on what one
Kansas City Baptist minister calls "situational ethics . . . no
concept of right and wrong." And discipline problems multiply as
a growing number of underclass youths spend more of their day at
school. A Maryland principal notes, "when the bell rings at three
o'clock not many kids leave, they hang around school as long as
they can . . . they've got no home to go home to."

"The kids who come from a deprived environment," says Dr.
Robert Blanc of the University of Missouri Medical School, "often
perceive their total environment as being unpredictable . . .
chaotic. And when they then go into a classroom, they're not
prepared to expect to find something that makes sense."

The desperate battle to educate underclass children weighs
heavily on the schools. Special programs—designed to raise expectations and confidence—have been helped by federal funds this
administration is now limiting. Where no programs exist, extra
time must be devoted to disadvantaged children—often at the
expense of those who are doing well. And in the Darwinian world
of school survival, by the time these students reach third grade they
have fallen even further behind.

If disadvantaged children don't get special, focused help in the
beginning grades, they are likely to sink steadily further behind. In
Kansas City, 25 percent of all junior high school students read
below a sixth grade level. But with inner-city schools themselves

19

struggling against financial duress, they can hardly supply that special effort to compensate for all students have missed at home.

A look at what this special help may accomplish may be glimpsed in Gregland Phillips who lives next door to his cousin, Dyshawn, in a frumpish quarter of Kansas City. As third graders, Dyshawn's reading level was one year behind his class, and Gregland still read at a first grade level. Their teacher, Linda Smith admitted that harried inner-city teachers simply didn't have the resources or the time to make a difference in the lives of children like Dyshawn and Gregland who arrive at school already seriously lagging.

"You retain them a year, and a lot of times that still is not enough to catch them up to their grade level. But when you have a whole classroom of children like this, of course, then they just become one in a crowd of children that you deal with."

In her hectic third-grade class, Linda Smith asks Gregland, sitting with other students around a table in the back of the room, to read a sentence from a large poster sheet: *The icy wind went right through my coat.* "Remember," she tells him, "*y* has an *e* sound."

Gregland, slumped listlessly to one side of the table, fretfully rubs an eye with his fingertips as he labors, "The . . . icy . . . wi . . . wi . . . wind . . . wuh . . . wuh . . ." It seems a hopeless and despairing toil against some stubborn barrier like an invisible pane of glass.

"You try to work with them on an independent basis," Linda Smith later reflects. "The time isn't there, and it becomes very difficult. We have a lot of children who come to school tired, they've been up late at night and haven't gone to sleep. And we, a lot of times, find that parents don't take the time to make sure that children get the proper amount of rest before coming to school."

Another child in her class, Saffiyah, a slight and wispy girl, passes much of the school day lying over her desk sleeping in the crook of her arm. Linda Smith makes occasional efforts to tug her awake, but Saffiyah only ruffles idly through pages of her text-book for a moment before dimming back to sleep. "It becomes a waste of time," says Miss Smith, "and even if she does sit up and is awake, she's not really listening. She's so tired that she is not going to be paying attention." So that a day at school for a child like Saffiyah, acknowledged Miss Smith, is a total blank. "And so if we've taught a new skill, she's lost out on the skill. . . ."

Later, out on the playground, Saffiyah explains that she is drowsy in class "because I went to bed late yesterday." When she comes to school, she says, "they just let us go to sleep."

The disorder in the home lives of disadvantaged children is reflected in their classrooms. For Linda Smith, it is daily a fitful and frenetic effort to preside over a ceaseless insubduable moil of children scuffling, strolling about, talking, abruptly leaving the classroom. They are used to doing what they want, when they want to do it," she says. "It becomes an impossibility, when kids are acting up, running around your classroom and not listening."

Repeatedly she tries to keep Dyshawn at his desk—"If you're not seated immediately, I'll go have Mr. Scott in here." Dyshawn—an elfin child with a bright sprawling grin—later describes it, "I'll be going around the classroom, helping people work. Go to the bathroom." He bolts up once to amble to the washroom in the back, where he stands before a mirror dabbling at his hair—"I put water on my hair . . . Acting like Michael Jackson. I'd like to be like Michael Jackson when I grow up to be a superstar." He then comes casually strutting back to this desk as Miss Smith cries, "Dyshawn, I *told* you. . . ."

She admitted that many children like Gregland and Dyshawn are, in all likelihood, already lost. "They become too far behind to catch up, and unless something miraculous occurs in their educational future, they will not succeed at all."

"If we don't find a way for them to catch up early," says Dr. Ernest Boyer, president of the Carnegie Foundation for the Advancement of Teaching, and once Secretary of Education under President Carter, "we're going to see this gap between the succeeders and the losers grow. And the reason that's a critical issue is, because we're an aging population overall. But the black and Hispanic families continue to populate the schools in large numbers. And that means, looking to America in the future, we're

21

going to have to find a way to include all of our children—or else, the failure rate will increase, and the vitality of this nation I think will decline.''

Some of the children can escape that pattern of defeat if they happen on the right school. Chauncy Coody is one such fortunate youngster—bused from his inner-city neighborhood to an integrated school in a middle-class community. Here—with fewer students per teacher, more individual attention, and, most importantly, an atmosphere of brisk optimism and expectations—Chauncy is performing at or above grade level. But it was only by chance he landed in that school.

And ''we can't count on chance to provide people with the kinds of experiences they need to be successful,'' says Dr. Comer of Yale. ''We need an institution within our society that very systematically teaches the children the skills necessary to be successful in the kind of complex age we live in today.''

There is now evidence that we do know how to salvage children from impoverished environments. A recent federal study showed that, over the last decade, nine-year-olds from disadvantaged families who attended schools with special federally-funded learning programs actually improved their reading scores at a rate *higher* than their counterparts in more affluent schools—though, still not rapidly enough to catch up.

Deep in one of Kansas City's derelict neighborhoods, Phillips Elementary School provides its disadvantaged students extra teachers and resources through a federal program called ''Follow Through.'' The principal at Phillips is Herman Gant, black, himself from a deprived home, a quiet-spoken but indeflectably resolute man who, standing outside his school one bright spring morning in dark glasses and a three-piece pastel peach suit, declared, ''We're not going to save them all, but that doesn't mean we're going to give up. . . .''

In one early-grade classroom inside, a teacher paces among youngsters clustered up and down long tables in an orderly and attentive calm that could not seem more remote from the tumult of many inner-city classrooms. ''Is there anyone who can go to the chalkboard?'' Hands flurry up around her. ''Vicky, would you go to the chalkboard and work it for us since you read? Six cats sat on a fence. Three cats ran away. How man cats were left sitting on the fence?'' Vicky happily bobs up—a plumpish little girl in a sundress, her hair pinched up into beribboned waggling pig-tails—and goes to the board, carefully picks up the chalk, and begins deliberately tracing a 6. ''That a nice six, Vicky,'' says the teacher behind her. . . .

''Regardless of deprivation,'' continued Herman Gant, ''all children *can* learn. But you must have high expectations for those young people at all times. And the teachers work very hard at giving them positive kinds of feedback.''

Standing close to the chalkboard, Vicky meticulously inscribes a *3*, then makes a line underneath, and, after a pause, slowly draws—a *2*. A collective hushed gasp arises from the class, and Vicky turns with an alarmed, uncertain look. ''Okay. That's all right,'' says the teacher. ''Now, Vicky, make a little picture by your problem. . . .''

''I tell all our young people as I go around and speak to them,'' concluded Gant, ''that they can be whatever they want to be. It doesn't matter where you come from, the kind of home that you have, whether you have a mother or father. It depends on you.''

Vicky, huddling close to the chalkboard, carefully scrubs out the 2 with the eraser. Pondering for a long moment, she then traces with a scrupulous deliberation—*3*. ''Now, give her a big hand,'' says the teacher, and there is a rustle of applause around the classroom, as Vicky turns to go back to her seat, biting her lower lip in a shy beam of pride. ''Vicky,'' says the teacher, ''you did a real good job. . . .''

In just that one small moment—that difference of numbers realized and corrected by Vicky—lay, in a sense, her hopes of defeating the world of despair around her. And that is the great drama—that slow, progressive dawning of light, of apprehension, of understanding—that is daily taking place in classrooms like Vicky's over the nation.

The children of poverty, it's now clear, *can* be rescued from the

23

cycle of defeat into which they were born. It would amount to an immense undertaking, no doubt—and one this country has not yet shown the will to confront. But it's an inescapable battle, as more and more disadvantaged children arrive at our school doors over the next decade.

And a battle especially critical for the kinds of children we have glimpsed here—children with little in their lives now. Except the same dreams of all our children.

Vicky: "I want to be a veterinarian when I grow up."

Chauncy softly murmurs: "I would like to be a lawyer."

Gregland: "I want to be a policeman when I grow up."

And Dyshawn, asked what he wants to be when he's grown, answers almost in a whisper, a slow smile stealing uncertainly over his face: "A science."

One spring morning in 1984, the students of Blair High, in Silver Spring, Maryland, thronged into the school auditorium for a rousing and tumultuous concert called "The Rock and Soul Review" —a cast of students performing their own blaring evocations of the music of the Fifties and early Sixties, a time which, to many of them, had to seem as distant and alien as another century: back before the Beatles, when Elvis was still young and a national mania, and snugly intact families gathered around black and white televisions to watch how Father Knew Best, and Beaver coming home from school to milk and cookies with Mom.

The nuclear family mythologized for a generation of baby boomers by "Leave It To Beaver" is fading as quickly as the receding image on a turned off television screen.

And what has happened to the American family since that cozily innocent time has profoundly transformed the mission of America's schools. A condition once thought peculiar to our cities' ghettoes—the disintegration of family life—is now quietly but massively spreading into the tidy refuges of middle- and working-class America, both black and white. Increased rates of divorce and births out of wedlock combined with soaring number of women in the work force have left many children—even those from financially secure homes—without the support and guidance the middle-class family has traditionally provided. These children are now coming to school less directed, less motivated. Increasingly, the schools are being forced to take on a parental role.

Fully a quarter of the students at Blair High now come from single-parent homes. Nationwide, the percentage of children living with only one parent has doubled since 1970. According to the latest Census Bureau survey, only 41 percent (25.1 million out of 61.4 million) of America's fathers have their children under the age of 18 living with them. In 1984, more than two-thirds of the mothers of school-age children now hold jobs, compared with about one-half in 1975. The traditional family—husband, wife staying home with children—has been reduced to only *a seventh* of America's households. And in well over half of America's families, both parents are working.

All that translates into more and more children left alone at home in the hours outside school, at ever-earlier ages. It is a widening social revolution in the country that promises to have an equally revolutionary effect on our schools over the next decade.

"Now, single-parent families and two parents working tend to be the rule, not the exception," says Dr. Boyer of the Carnegie Foundation, "which means the school is dealing with the child more independently than in the past. And more than that, I think in the future, the schools will have to have what perhaps might be called a custodial role. I mean by that, they're going to have to take on more responsibility for the life of the child if the parent is engaged outside the home."

Like any social revolution, the freedom recently opened to women to work outside the home has carried an unanticipated toll: a growing population of children thrown on their own outside school—in effect, day-orphans—now a fourth of our elementary school enrollment. They have come to be termed "latch-key children." On every school day, an estimated six-and-a-half million children under twelve years old come home to let themselves into empty houses, no one there to help with homework, or even to see that they do it. By dinnertime, parents are often too spent from work to help them study, to give them the close attention and encouragement so vital to a child's performance in school, especially during their early years. From homes empty of that focus and care, they come to school thus empty, unsure, far less motivted to learn.

Latch-key children present schools with a new gallery of problems. Children with no one at home can't be sent home sick. They are tardy and absent more often than those with a parent home during the day. And many parents with latch-key children are expecting schools to do even more. In Montgomery County— while some factions are pushing to lower school taxes—other parents are demanding all-day kindergarten, not so much for an academic return as for simple public supported custodial care.

"The latch-key experience," says Lynette Long of the National Institute on Latch-Key Children, "is one of the major crises to hit the educational system in this decade. Maybe the most major. Some students fare very well; other students cannot cope with self-care. I see it as the hub of a wheel with problems radiating. We're talking about the mainstream U.S.A. here."

For over a year now, Ian Baldwin—a freckled and sandy-haired ten-year-old—has walked from school to his house in a neatly groomed suburban neighborhood in Maryland's Montgomery County, pausing at the front door to carefully unfasten the keys pinned inside the flap of his book satchel, entering then the hush of a home with no one else there. He pours himself a glass of orange juice from the refrigerator. "Then I get something to eat. It feels pretty big, getting to go home alone, getting to sort of run the house."

He will occupy himself for a while, leaning forward on the edge of the sofa, intently playing a maze game with ball and flippers, its quiet clacking the only sound around him. "At first I think I was sort of not used to it, with all the silence and all. And I got really scared."

He sometimes seeks to fill the silence, even when he turns to his homework, with the noise of a radio, or just the continual murmur of a running television set. "It sort of keeps me company. And sometimes when I don't watch T.V. or play the radio, I mean sometimes it doesn't really help and I get lonely sometimes, you know, and sometimes it gets kind of boring."

What, he is asked, does the term "latch-key child" mean?

"I'm not really sure. It just means you stay at home and," he ventures with a wistful tilt of his head, an uneasy little smile, "you're under a latch and key."

Ian was still doing good work in school. But the latch-key phenomenon is so recent, major studies to measure its magnitude and effects are only now under way. Educators themselves—principals, teachers, superintendents—report that latch-key problems of absenteeism, undone homework, insecurities distracting concentration, have become one of the most staggering challenges facing their schools.

There are certain subtle, statistically elusive consequences of the increasing ranks of latch-key children and children from single-parent families. When one-half of the family-school equation breaks down, academic performance seems to falter. With less parental supervision, less time is spent on homework, more time on T.V. Adult monitoring of a child's school performance becomes more distant, haphazard, desultory. Several experts, including Dr. John Goodlad and Dr. Amati Etzioni, feel that the new prominence of single-parent homes (and/or youths with busy working mothers) is so profound a change in our society that schools in the coming decade will have to formally institute curriculum additions to teach the basic human and personality development once learned in the family.

Already there is evidence of this change. In Maryland, state requirements now call for schools to include the study of "values." Even the school prayer controversy can be seen in terms of parents who desire the school to take on the more personal development tasks once covered by the dwindling nuclear family.

At Takoma Park Junior High School in Maryland—where 85 percent of the student body is from poor or working class single-parent homes—the school is kept open into the evening to provide adult supervision not only for junior high youths, but also for the

27

younger brothers and sisters so often in their care. At Bathesda's Walt Whitman High—ranked one of the best schools in the country—seminars for troubled single parents have become a part of this upper-middle-class school's services.

"I think this is something that has not been sufficiently thought about in American education or in American life," proposes Dr. Robert Coles, child psychiatrist with Harvard University. "And I fully understand why men and women both want to work and *need* to work, and I fully understand the social pressures as well as the economic pressures. But I do wonder what it means to children to come home from school and find no adult there."

Increasingly, latch-key children are found to be from the sort of families customarily thought to be the most supportive of schools, moderately affluent and excellently educated. Thus, the nurturing family—once a vital historical link between school and home—is dissolving. In Montgomery County, Maryland, in fact, the higher the educational level of both parents, the higher the odds of them having latch-key children.

Sophie Shive was eight years old, a second grader, in the spring of 1984. Her mother works in a bank, her father is completing a Ph.D. in Greek studies. Walking home after school along the quiet and leafy streets of a pleasant Montgomery County neighborhood, Sophie never knows whether she'll find someone at home or not when she gets there. "I like it better when someone's there," she confides, in the smallest wisp of a voice, as faint and tremulous as a brief stirring of grass. A slight, wan girl with a porcelain-delicate seraphic face, she has strangely ashen eyes, a gaze somehow remote, abstracted. At times, when no one's in the house, she's unable to get in. "If it's locked, I don't get in. I try all the doors first." She will then retreat into her log-wall playhouse in the backyard, or climb into the high branches of a dogwood tree in her front yard. There she will wait—in the swimming shadows of its leaves, alone—until someone returns home.

Her father explains, "If she finds a door open, she can go in and ring up her mother. What she usually does, though, is goes about playing in the yard or in her room. And I often find her asleep in her

28

room when I get back. . . . Asleep. That's one way to deal with free time, with solitude.''

Found one spring afternoon curled into her playhouse, silently arranging inscrutable little totems of miscellaneous scraps and tufts, she was asked what she was doing. She answered after a moment, a barely audible breath: ''Making secrets.''

''To me,'' says Dr. Coles, ''one of the most important parts of my experience going through school was having my mother home and having her reinforce what I learned in school. But when both parents are gone, whether it be in the first grade or the tenth grade, you wonder what effect this is going to have on children. I'll tell you, I think a very sad and bad effect.''

To deal with some of the fears and anxieties of children left alone with responsibilities beyond their age, a telephone emergency line for latch-key children has been set up in Montgomery County—one of 200 such services across the country. Throughout one raining afternoon last year, a roomful of women softly answered a scattered ringing of phones, as thunder intermittently blustered outside the blurring windows. Through that dim and dully thundering afternoon, it was a poignant and continuing chorus of calls coming from unseen solitary children in unseen rooms across the community.

''You're afraid of the storm? Where are you? . . . What do you usually do when they're home and it's storming?''

''You sound like you were crying . . . Just a little? Did you hurt yourself? . . . You hurt your knee. Did you fall?''

''So you have no idea what time they're coming home? And there's no way to know how long the storm's going to last. . . . Do you feel safer just talking to somebody? You do. . . . Have you ever talked to your parents about being scared? . . . You haven't.''

Inevitably, such anxieties are impinging on these children's performances in school. ''Children who experience a great deal of fear,'' says Lynette Long, ''and one out of four latch-key children do—to a child who goes home to an empty house who's frightened enough to hide in a closet or under a bed—at one o'clock you start thinking, 'Is it safe to walk home? What about opening the door?'

29

all of those things loom larger than life, and the child is distracted in school.''

At least one recent study has already found a nine-point drop in achievement scores among elementary children whose mothers work full-time. And often, latch-key children—because no one's home in the morning—simply don't show up for school at all. ''The children that are home alone in the morning many times will miss the bus,'' says Mrs. Long. No one's there to wake them up, get them ready. Or even if they're up, they'll decide they don't want to go to school, so they'll call their parent at work and say, 'Oh, I don't feel so great.'''

At the same time, some children arrive at school sick, because no one's home to tend to them. Lynette Long and her husband, Thomas, also found, even in affluent areas, a problem with proper nourishment. ''About a fourth of all children show up in the morning without having had breakfast,'' says Thomas Long. ''That's a real negative impact on their ability to learn during the course of the day.''

As more and more of these children spill into our schools, it will increasingly fall to those schools to compensate for the absence of care at home. In fact, the problem is becoming so urgent and imposing, it has compelled the first major reconsideration of the nine-month school calendar since its original design for America's early farming society. Several states are beginning to seriously study the option of bringing children into school earlier, keeping them there longer, by expanding both the school day and the school year. Necessarily, that will also greatly expand the burdens on our schools.

Dr. Goodlad suggests, ''Now, with millions of children being latch-key children, coming home to nobody, the changing demographics have strengthened, if anything, the need for a school which provides a surrogate parent role, and in effect, an educating babysitting role.''

Declares Dr. Boyer, ''We're also talking about extending the school day, not for educational reasons, but because parents aren't home to care for them. On the one hand, we say: let's narrow the goals of schools, let's go back to the new basics the National Commission talks about—make them academically more rigorous. Down here, however, there's a shift in this society in which the parents expect the schools to carry on a social, custodial function, as well as an academic one.

"So, to put it bluntly, we're talking out of both sides of our mouths."

3. The Tribal World of the Young

As we've already seen, the old centers of gravity in American life—secure family, secure community—are fast disappearing. As if to fill that emptiness, many young people, by high school, dwell in a restless clamor of diversions—television, rock, drugs. Unlike distractions of the past, this new weather of preoccupations is profoundly shifting the way our youth learn more toward sheer random sensation and experience, alienating them from the measured processes of the classroom, inevitably degrading their performance there.

—Television. By graduation, many students will have spent five thousand more hours in front of a television screen than before a teacher.
—Drugs, alcohol. Once thought a blight particular to the ghettoes of the poor, they are now pervasive throughout our schools, including those in that other ghetto of the Great American Suburbia.
—Even jobs. In part to afford their other diversions, more students are now working much longer hours than before, further eroding their concentration on school.

As an example, we will focus on a school, and students, in a middle-class area of Los Angeles—among those immense suburban flatlands in the murky and nebulous sunlight of that seasonless place at the continent's far edge where a migratory and pastless population dwells among expressway winds of ceaseless speed,

31

and from which, through decades of television sit-coms and action dramas set among its low level boulevards under tall stilts of palm trees, the nation has come by a peculiar Southern California image of itself. More, it is out there, where the land ends, that there seems forever emerging what the rest of the nation is next becoming. What we find in the students there may be a flashier reflection of what, nevertheless, is true of students across the country.

Monroe High School sits amid the limitless suburban plains of the San Fernando Valley. A compound of barracks-like classroom buildings neatly ranked within wire fences around a quadrangle of closely clipped grass, it vaguely resembles some Air Force base suspended in a bright-hazed void, a drowsing lassitude over its sunny grounds.

In the parking lot there one May afternoon in 1984, a week before Monroe High's graduation prom, a solitary student on a skateboard skimmed and floated through other students milling and lounging among their cars, dressed in a haphazard harlequin variety, Deerslayer leggings, bandanas, rainbowed tee-shirts, a few with savagely scissored sprays of hair dyed in Easter-chick colors, some sunbathing on car hoods with radios beating in the air—a small, casual glimpse of the world now of America's young. A world increasingly estranged from school.

"There's a lot of people psyched up about the prom," said Rachel Hughes, a senior. "That's all they talk about."

The final bell for the day released an uproar of motorbikes, cars, churning out of the school's lots. Among them, in an old but carefully burnished blue coupe, was Danny, a senior, mustachioed, wind blowing his long hair about his shoulders as he drove along a wide avenue with his girlfriend, Sheila, glisteningly pretty with radiant eloquent eyes. "Are you gonna study for that test?" Danny asked her.

"Yeah, yeah," she sighed. It was an idle, absent patter as they wheeled free along spacious boulevards to whunking rock on the car radio.

"That's good," said Danny. "You gotta get a B on that thing, at least."

She gave him a quick, sharp look. "Does that mean you're not gonna come over and study with me?"

"I might. You got a lot more studying to do than I do, though . . . I only got one hard final, you got three hard finals."

"So what?" said Sheila, with a stealthy smile beginning to curl. "All I'm worried about is getting past second. 'Cause first period is no big deal, really. There's nothing for me to study. . . ." She paused. "And fifth period," she turned to Danny and grinned, "I'm just gonna guess," touching then the tip of her tongue to her upper lip and giving it a delicate little naughty nip.

Danny chortled. "Oh, great. . . ."

At first glance, it may all seem—cars, dates, dances, music—an evocation of earlier high school days, a common memory of us all. But for increasing numbers of America's youth, a different reality lies behind those familiar appearances: a pop-electronic tribal culture that has become for them *all* of life, with school itself a distraction. They dwell almost completely in the electronic pulse of the instant, isolated from any larger sense of the world, without any larger memory of the past.

"We care about our future, we don't care about the past," said one Monroe High student at a late afternoon beer party amid blarings of punk rock. "The Revolutionary War? That's over with. We want to know what's gonna happen to *us*. Math? I don't know, 'cause I mean, what job uses math besides—if you want to use it, go ahead. I mean, find a job. But I mean, construction workers don't—I don't know any construction workers that really use algebra."

Rachel Hughes, a huskily handsome girl with crystal-strand earrings under long crisping curls, whose mother is divorced, cheerfully allowed, "When I get home, I won't have time to do my homework. I like to be active when I get home. I like to do different kinds of sports—run, gynmastics, dance, swim, dive. . . ." But principally, the lives of Rachel and her friends seemed focused on television—languorous afternoons, diving into turquoise backyard pools, that are strangely merged with the unreality of television commercials and their dream visions: *A golden life. And I will feel*

33

this way forever. . . . *Share the fantasy.* "I watch a lot of television," says Rachel. "A lot. Cartoons in the morning, get ready for school. Then I watch my soap operas, and then I watch what's ever on at night." Collected on a back patio around a television set, she and her sunny-haired friends seem almost to exist in some alter-world indistinguishable from that behind the screen they are raptly watching: *You don't really think I bought that buddy-buddy friendship between you and Ray, do you?* . . . *I never said I was Ray's buddy, you must have gotten that from.* . . . *You've destroyed the lives of everybody that's been in touch with you. You've used them.* . . . If anything, it's as if that mirage world contained in the window of television is more intense, actually more alive, than their own reality—as if, in fact, *they* were the illusion: "Celia thinks that Grant tried to murder her, and Grant was her husband, right? But it was really the other Grant that was doing all this."

"I know," says Rachel, "'cause he set a bomb in that boat."

"And Tanya's in love with Grant."

"Who's Tanya?"

"The lady that works at the hospital with the bald haircut?"

"With the bald haircut?" giggles Rachel.

Many teachers feel the visual-audio world of television has disarrayed concentration in students, depredating verbal and written skills, scattering structured thought.

These teachers feel themselves placed in almost hopeless competition with the high-dazzle commotion of commercial television. Imparting complex and often difficult ideas is made even more trying with children conditioned to the quick and hectic rush of the video pageant.

Just how television affects learning is still being vigorously debated. Marie Winn surveyed American families for her book *The Plug In Drug,* and found that the average preschooler watches an average of fifty-four hours of television a week. But among deprived children, moderate viewers of television actually show improved achievement scores, according to a recent major study by the California Department of Education. That study also found that students who were heavy viewers of T.V. had lower achievement scores in reading, writing, and math. Still, defenders of television point out that studies have indicated that students with lower IQs also tend to watch more television—so that IQ, not simply heavy T.V. viewing, may be the real cause for lowered achievement scores.

Nevertheless, teachers and educational authorities consulted for ABC News' survey of America's public school system in 1984 contended that television can lead not only to shorter attention spans in the classroom, but can become a major distraction from homework and reading time. Whatever television's effects, one national study discovered that the number of people between the ages of 16 and 21 who had read even a fraction of a book during a year had dropped by 12 percent since 1978—to 63 percent now of that age group.

"I don't even remember the last book I read," Rachel conceded. "I really—the last book I read was a health book," and she gave a light skitter of a laugh.

"I don't read," another Monroe High student offered, a pert thatch-haired blonde working after school in a shopping mall boutique, as was a bower of dolls, selling stuffed toy animals. "You're gonna make me look like a dumb blonde, right? Okay," she nodded with a game smile, "Good. Good."

"I rarely read books outside of class," said Laura, a senior, and then added with her own quick little chuckle, "unless they're Harlequin romances or something that's really gushy."

Something about them in these professions, in their abashed and uneasily snickering blankness, oddly and touchingly suggested overgrown eight-year-olds, discovered to be still arrested in a careless childhood unknowing.

"The last book I read?" pondered Ron Robinson, the senior class president, and admitted after a moment with an embarrassed grin, "It's tough. . . ."

"Who me?" said Danny, with the same vaguely startled, bemused smile. "Probably *The Call of the Wild* when I was in sixth grade," which provoked from Sheila a delighted, delicious throaty

35

CHAPTER I

breath of a laugh.

Many teachers report they are finding in their students not only a growing alienation from books, but a deeper, more troubling impatience with the sequenced patterns of thought and written language itself. Television, says one, seems to be producing "students who have an attention span that's no longer than twenty minutes. Because at the end of that time, there's a commercial—they can get up, walk away." Now, the latest development in the pop-electronic storm, rock video—an almost total explosion of structured, connected thought into swirls of pure, pre-verbal, impressionistic sensation—is available to some students 24 hours a day.

According to a study just published in which children were tracked for six years, from preschool into elementary school, "Children who have spent more time watching television and especially the more violent programming, are less likely to show the self-restraint required to sit quietly for several minutes." When these findings are combined with those of the California surveys, it becomes clear that, at the least, teachers today face a terrific struggle against the allure and excitement of television.

"When you describe students who have never read a book," says Dr. Ravitch, "you're describing what is called today *a*literacy—people who know how to read and don't want to." She continues, "Television can be a very subversive aspect of education, not only because it is a passive medium, but because it encourages children not to do anything else. School requires you to work, and it requires input from the individual. And sometimes you don't do very good work, and the teacher says, 'You'll have to do that over again.' Television never makes you do anything over again. It gives you just what you want when you want it, and that's very narcisstic."

Studies of influences on the behavior of youths aged thirteen to nineteen—conducted in 1960 and 1980—revealed that the effect of peers and the electronic media was rising, while the influence of teachers and parents on their lives was declining. That pattern shows no evidence of abating. Rather, it threatens to draw the next

36

decade of students even further into an alienation from the classroom, forming a virtually impassible barrier between the nation's children, and the schools which are supposed to shape them.

But teenagers' self-absorption, their detachment from the classroom, is due to more than heavy television viewing. Drugs and alcohol are blurring the attention of our youth in school. Nationally, more than 40 percent of all high school students have at least tried marijuana, 35 percent have experimented with stimulants. And 16 percent have used cocaine.

James P. Comstock, Program Manager of San Francisco's Adolescent Care Unit reported: "The front line of the fight against drug addiction is the fifth and sixth grades." Moreover, what distinguishes this new group of abusers from those of an earlier generation of abusers is "polyabuse"—a term which describes those who mix drugs and alcohol or more than one chemical substance. Not only is such an addiction more lethal, it is more difficult to cure. Comstock continues: "By adolescence it's too late. Once the juices start flowing, they can't hear you."

Rachel Hughes says, "If you, like, take coke, you're all amped, you're jumping around, you're causing problems, and you're attracting everybody else's attention, and avoids them from doing their work. . . ." As for marijuana, "that makes you—it makes me sleepy, and you just sit there and you just veg. You just sit there and zone out on something, and you just—you burn out. You just get really tired, and then you really feel like don't doing anything."

It is not always the worst students who are the heaviest drug users. And while overall teenage drug use has stabilized or declined slightly in the past year, it has done so from peak levels that are hardly reassuring. Further, an alarmingly high 41 percent of high school seniors in the latest survey from the National Institute on Drug Abuse reported "binge drinking" or five or more drinks in a row within the two weeks previous to the survey. More than 25 percent of high school youths surveyed reported smoking marijuana regularly in the month prior to the National Institute on Drug Abuse study. Drug use has held to disturbingly high levels at some of the richer—and supposedly better—schools where students

37

have more money to spend. In ten middle class Los Angeles area high schools, the LAPD confiscated $49,500 worth of illegal drugs last year in an undercover sweep.

Such students—disconnected from their families and schools, from feelings of belonging or responsibility, insulated in their counter-culture—drift ever further from our society's goal of an educated populace. Often they become victims of their own illusions of beauty and glamour—.

Studies of influences on the behavior of youths aged thirteen to nineteen which were conducted in 1960 and 1980 revealed that the influence of peers and the electronic media was rising, while the influence of teachers and parents on their lives was declining.

Concentration, memory, alertness—all dimmed by drugs and alcohol. Those drugs and alcohol can be readily found wherever students congregate, including one of their most popular gathering grounds now—the shopping mall, that high sanctuary of suburbia, a constant noiseless glide of escalators up through the sun blurs of enclosed atriums in a quiet anesthesial murmur of music, past levels gardened like the terraces of Babylon, with their galleries of record stores and sportswear shops, ice cream and snack counters, video arcades, all offering a panorama of the culture of the young in America's consumer civilization. Many simply linger for hours among its cafe tables, its promenade benches, gazing vacantly about, smoking. The manager of a yogurt bar at one mall declared, "There's a few that are here all night long, until the mall closes. I've seen the exact same kids here, every day." One senses, he went on, that the shopping mall has replaced their homes as the center of their lives outside school.

Beyond its diversions, the shopping mall reflects another problem for schools: the increasing number of teenagers working there. In one boutique, Laura, a Monroe High senior, acknowledges, "I work approximately 23 hours a week—put designs on shirts, sell shirts, and lots of Michael Jackson. Everyone works."

According to one government study, 67 percent of high school students are now in the general workforce. With more students

38

working longer hours, jobs have become, for many, a fundamental subversion of school. Says Stanford University professor Gary Sykes, "This recent phenomenon of students working is a highly mixed blessing. On the one hand, students are learning a great deal about the world of work. On the other hand, the quantity and quality of their academic work in high school is suffering as a result of that."

Tony, another Monroe student, was employed by a 24-hour convenience store, operating the cash register at the check-out counter, loading bags, wheeling in shopping carts from the parking lot, from the late afternoon on through the long weary neon burn of the night. "My hours are sometimes six to midnight, or six to one o'clock in the morning," he said. "Even if I do make it to school the next day, I'm really burnt out, and I can't function very well at school. I only go to school three days a week on the average. Sometimes I don't go to classes, I'll oversleep because of work. I look at myself as being sort of a part-time student in a full-time school." A serious and neatly trimmed youth, Tony observed in a flat, toneless voice, "It's helped a lot to become an adult. But sometimes you miss a part of being a kid by working so much, and missing out on a lot of things."

All these distractions—drugs, television, work, with the disintegration of family life—have contributed to an increase in students simply not showing up for classes: "ditching," as students commonly term it. One national poll found that fully half of seniors reported cutting classes.

"I'm failing all my classes," admitted one Monroe student, a freckled and waifish girl, "due to the fact that I don't go to school. I go, but I've missed quite a few days."

Ron, the senior class president, confided, "I have better things to do, and school's pretty easy for me right now, so," he grinned, "I ditch a lot. You know, I mean, like today. I'm ditching today. I came to school, but I didn't go to school—you know what I mean?"

Leaning with one arm on his car, Danny whimsically explained, "I wanted to get out of school so bad to get home and work on my

39

car, and then when I get my car done, I want to go out and drive it.''
Asked if now, on the point of graduation, he feels he derived as
much from high school as he could have, he answers with a jaunty
resignation, ''As I could have? No, probably not.''

But Sheila, sitting in the opened door below him, seemed to have
more misgivings about that. ''Looking back, yes, I would do it all
over, I'd get better study habits, keep up my grades, and go to class
a little bit more often. Because—'' and she paused to lift her
necklace loop thoughtfully to her teeth and bite it uneasily, ''—I
screwed up a lot during the last year, last years, when I shouldn't
have. . .'' She gave a wistful half-smile. ''But I did.''

In fact, the counter-classroom culture is now claiming so much
of students' lives, it may challenge the fundamental nature and idea
of schooling itself over the next decade.

Says Dr. Boyer of the Carnegie Foundation, ''I believe the
stimulation, the distractions, the perhaps premature confidence
that children and young people establish in the culture today puts
the school and the classroom on the defensive. They've acquired so
much that the school perhaps is seen as almost a distraction in their
lives. Now, that's always been true to some extent, but I think in
the last 10 to 20 years, that's clearly the dramatic trend. Looking
ahead, the question remains will the school be the primary teacher—or will the nonformal teachers be dominant? I mean by that,
television, magazines, videocassettes, records, radios, travel,
peers. These are the places where the sources of knowledge increasingly are for our children. So the question is, will the school
become increasingly dreary and obsolete, and will young people
feel more and more alienated in this process, while they rely more
and more on the informal teachers beyond the classroom that they
depend on because they're spending more time with them?''

At Monroe High the week before the prom, ditching acceler-
ated. Halls and classrooms began to appear already evacuated for
the summer.

''*No one's* coming to school on Friday,'' said Laura. ''*Everyone's* preparing for the prom.''

Said Tony, "This is the big night of the year. . . ."

Finally, on May 25th, 1984, in a golden southern Califorma dusk, the graduates of Monroe High gathered for their prom, arriving in a steady flowing shimmer and purr of rented limousines beneath the vast corporate-imperial glimmering of Century Plaza, spilling out into the warm lavendar-and-apricot Los Angeles twilight in pastel tuxedoes and ruffled shirts and gauzy gowns to observe the ceremonial end of their twelve-year journey through public school, and more, the final formal end of their childhood. . . . In a cavernous ballroom of crimson and gilt, as they danced, clustered, whispered, duskily lit in candleglow, they seemed somehow still suspended in a curious and poignant innocence. Directly ahead of them now awaited the inevitability of the larger, more complicated and demanding world—a world more rigorous and unforgiving than most of them possibly could imagine, that imminent future still little more to them than a dream on this last luminous evening of celebration.

But a dream for a few of them, vaguely troubled—by suspicions that, in all the music and diversions of their own communal culture, they might have missed something vital in school, never to be recovered now. Knowledge and understandings that enlarge life. Skills to prepare them for what was immediately ahead. A disquiet that, in fact, they might find themselves lost in that wider, daylit world into which they would suddenly awake tomorrow.

"Your social life, your friends," mused Tony, "it all plays a real important role. It makes this big thick blanket that surrounds you. It suddenly all comes to an end like it is now. It leaves you a little scared. . . . It's all up to you what you do. And if you mess up, you're history."

Lured by drugs and alcohol, unengaged by the schools which are supposed to educate them, it is no wonder so many students drop out of school altogether. It is the ultimate disconnection.

Students who have poor grades, who are enrolled in non-academic programs, or who come from poorer school backgrounds are the most likely to leave school. American Indians and natives of Alaska have the highest drop-out rates, followed by Hispanics and black students. These students, the ones whose futures are already most at risk, drop out in massive numbers. Twenty-five percent of our high school youth nationally—approaching 50 percent in many urban centers and 40 percent or more in Louisiana and both Carolinas—eventually leave without diplomas.

The question of how to salvage them may be America's most urgent educational problem, and perhaps its most difficult to solve. The National Center for Educational Statistics revealed that many high school drop-outs are still unemployed two years or more after leaving. The tragedy of these poorly-motivated, low-achieving young people is seldom addressed, often left a shadow phenomenon. Yet their failure is a national failure.

Frighteningly, many students who turn off harbor intense angers and resentments, which they express by turning on those around them—those they perceive, and sometimes rightly so, as having failed them. On January 24 of 1984, the White House released a new federal report dealing with the topic of disorder in the public schools, which stated: "We believe that the problems of school disorder are perhaps the most overlooked civil-rights issues of the 1980s." According to the annual Gallup Poll on education, in all but one of the last fifteen years, discipline has been ranked as the number one problem in the schools.

In some of those schools across America, pupils "shoot up" on the stairwells—snorting coke and smoking pot, carrying switchblades and ghetto blasters. There are brutal assaults inside classrooms as well, such as one in New York which left teacher, Howard Sauerhoff, with a battered face, and the recent raping of a schoolgirl while students cheered.

The percentage of teachers polled by the National Education Association who reported being physically attacked increased by 53 percent between 1977 and 1983. And the percentage reporting malicious damage to their property increased by 63 percent over the same period. More than 250,000 students were physically attacked each month. Two-and-a-half million were victims of thefts.

There were 2,730 violent incidents in New York schools during

1981-82. Detroit administrators are trying to prevent any future violence of the kind that in 1983 resulted in the shooting of a youth outside a high school. In Los Angeles last year, arson, vandalism and thefts cost the district nearly six million dollars.

According to Dr. Herbert Pardes, Director of the National Institute on Mental Health, one in eight high school teachers "hesitates to confront students out of fear." Such fear is widespread:

Not long ago, in the deep green summer shade of a spacious New Jersey home, nine-year-olds splashed in a toy-cluttered pool, watched by Lesley, a soft-spoken girl with warm brown eyes and daisy-petaled lashes. Working during the summertime as a nanny, Lesley is a student teacher from Trenton State College. "I couldn't believe it when I got back here," she said in her soft, incredulous voice. "The children actually listen. At the school to which I've been assigned in Trenton, my main job is to keep the children from seriously injuring each other. I try to teach second grade. The oldest child is ten and incorrigible. Some can hardly speak. Most bite, kick and steal from each other all day. When I try to stop them, they go after me."

Our public schools must be freed from the spectre of violence if they are to have any chance of reviving. How to do that remains one of the most intractable difficulties confronting us today. But there's no question that concern about violence is a primary source of the waning public faith in our schools.

PART II

The Perilous Decade:

TEACHERS

4. The Imperiled Profession

No single protagonist is so immediately central to the nation's hopes for saving its public school system as the teacher. The teachers in our classrooms are on the front line—as the vital point of contact, as the transmitting synapse and actualization—in the whole struggle to revive our schools. But as we enter the next decade, teaching itself has become an imperiled profession. Those to whom we've entrusted the growth and preparation of our children's minds are themselves caught in an alarming pattern of professional decline toward mediocrity and incompetence. The renewal of American public education greatly depends on reversing the decay of teaching.

But that process of decay promises to grow graver. Increasingly forbidding conditions—meager pay, overloaded classes, overwhelming responsibilities, oppressive bureaucracy, little esteem from society—are inexorably eroding both the numbers and the quality of our teachers. The best, losing the heart and will to continue, are abandoning the classroom to those less able. In pockets across the country, teacher shortages are already developing. In the coming decade, a national shortage is predicted. At the same time, fewer and more dubious prospects are coming into teaching. The schools of education, the teachers of our teachers, are themselves becoming academic wastelands which, as

47

enrollments dwindle, lower their standards to keep their class-rooms populated. Moreover, once the teachers issuing from these institutions graduate into the classroom, they find themselves isolated, with little feedback or response; and evaluation proce-dures for those needing help are a meaningless ritual. It is almost impossibly complicated, time-consuming, contentious, and ex-pensive ever to flush out even the most clearly unfit among them. Teachers' unions, in their grim battle to improve the Dickensian conditions of teaching, have often seemed to the public eye to resort to the intransigent, the overly defensive, the irresponsibly self-serving—allergic to any fundamental reform. Fairly or not, this has further degraded the general image of teachers, from one of dedicated professionals to that of just another special interest lobby.

All of these factors have converged into a critical moment for the future of teaching. The fear is that, if these tendencies continue over the next decade, our teaching cadre could become so en-feebled, it will produce a student generation lost in its time, and lead to the slow-motion collapse of the very validity of, and national belief in, our entire public school system.

At a moment of desperate need for able teachers—with a na-tional concern over student test scores, with many schools floun-dering, an atmosphere of despair, anger, exhaustion, and desertion has settled over our teaching corps itself. More than half the country's teachers say they would not choose teaching if they had to do it over again. Twenty years ago, only 11 percent indicated they felt that way. In other words, over half the nation's teachers would like to forsake their chosen vocation: a stunning testimonial of disillusionment. Forty percent declare they're leaving their classrooms before retirement. And it's usually the most able—the most earnest, the brightest—who are inclined to leave.

As a result, the surplus of teachers which prevailed in the Seventies has now, in the late Eighties, suddenly become a short-age. Thirty-eight states already have a serious deficit of math and science teachers, and almost 8 percent of all high school math-ematics and science teachers, according to the National Science

Board, have left the classroom for industry. Of those who are left, over half have been judged unqualified by their principals. What's more, the shortage threatens to grow even worse. Albert Shanker projects that, over the next decade, we will have to replace two-thirds of our teaching force. But replace them with whom? For the very reasons driving so many teachers out of the classroom, even fewer promising potential teachers are attracted in to take their place. Enrollment in teacher education schools has dropped by 50 percent over the last decade.

"We are looking at about 1200 to 1400 teachers short for next year," admitted Ronald Diaz, director of central personnel for the Los Angeles system. "By the end of this decade we could be six thousand to eight thousand teachers short."

All of this comes into an urgent sun-lens focus in Los Angeles. For students there who hope for a meaningful education and who, with their parents, believe education is the window to a wider future, the situation is approaching disaster:

Six hundred classrooms were unfilled during 1984 because there were no teachers to teach in them. In 1985 that number will swell to 1500.

There are shortages in every specialty except art and physical education.

Nine hundred and fifty classes are taught by teachers with "emergency credentials." Fully half of these teachers have been unable to meet state requirements, and will be read out of the system next year.

The city will need about 9000 new teachers by 1990 but two-thirds of those applying for teaching jobs flunk the entry level competency test.

In California, half of the teaching force is over 50 years old and will retire in a decade. The state will need 150,000 new teachers; but at Berkeley, ten students choose the Peace Corps for every one who chooses teaching.

The toll of all this on the children has been incalculable.

TO SAVE OUR SCHOOLS

At Parmalee Elementary School, the inner city school where gifted teacher Jill Baim taught, children, from the surrounding grim warren of streets, would begin to collect and stand waiting behind the locked gates of the school, in the gray still morning, fully an hour before the first bell of the day. Finally, they would be released into the schoolyard, calls and trills of Spanish rippling over the grounds. Among them was class number forty-four—a fifth grade class with no permanent teacher and some fifteen substitute teachers during that year. Each morning when the pupils of class forty-four set out for school, they could not be certain who their teacher would be—or even if one would show up. They had become, in effect, orphans of the system. One particular morning at Parmalee, eleven teachers were absent, with not enough substitutes to take their places—and once again, class forty-four arrived at school to find no teacher to take them in. They were left to wander about the schoolyard for some twenty minutes. "Every day we come to school, we don't know who's our teacher," said Maria, pretty, bright-faced, with dark eager eyes, dressed in a crisply-starched ruffled dress. "We think it's going to be Mr. Frank, and sometimes it's not him—it's another teacher who gives us kindergarten work. We feel bad, 'cause nobody wants to be our real teacher, like nobody cares for us or nothing."

Small as they were, the children of class forty-four seemed all too aware of the damage being done then. "This year I haven't been learning nothing," said Ricardo. "Last year, I learned some of my times tables, and now I forgot them, because—I don't know them now." Said Maria, "They give us first-grade work, and we don't like to do first-grade work. We like to do fifth- and sixth-grade work, so we could learn, and when we grow up we could get a job."

Finally, class forty-four was collected from the schoolyard and conducted into their room, where they sat with vacant uncertain faces as a supervising teacher, Tina Patterson, told them, "Mr. Frank is not here today, and so you guys have to be divided. All right?" They were then distributed among other classes in the

50

school, some of them in first grade rooms. One teacher who had taken in class forty-four children other times was Jill Baim, who reported that when she gave them homework along with her own fourth graders, every one of them brought it in the next morning, however crudely done—and when they left her class after another teacher was found for them, some would return to her for two or three days afterward, asking her to give them homework again.

Jill Baim, a young, brisk, compact teacher, with large luminous eyes—went about shutting up her fourth-grade classroom, at Parmalee Elementary School closing lockers, gathering her papers, at the end of another school day. "Since I was in kindergarten," she said, "I wanted to teach. And all through my schooling, I went to school to become a teacher." Jill Baim—full of a seemingly indefatigable energy and vibrancy—was quitting the classroom, harried out by institutional frustrations, a mounting sense of futility.

"I'm leaving because I'm not able to teach effectively and give the children quality education," she confessed. "I just don't think the system works. And I am part of that system. I don't like being part of the system that doesn't work.

She is abandoning, after only three years in the classroom, that long dream of hers—her spirit too beleaguered by the paperwork of bureaucratic regulations, by the contempt she feels around her for the profession, but most of all by the baffling chasm interposed between what she is allowed to give her children and what she knows they really need. Her decision, it is clear, is still anguishing for her. She finished her last days as a teacher with a certain harried and hectic raggedness, sometimes a bit brittle and shrill with her students. Yet there remained hints of the gift she had obviously had: the rare and indispensible art of inspired teaching. During recess, several students would come to her as she sat in the classroom and would sit close to her as she patiently read to them from books they handed her.

Her fourth-graders, recalling what she had taught them—"How to grow up and learn things, how to be proud, how to be a man, how to go in life without quitting, how to do things you've never done before''—would burst into tears. Each time Jill recalled what she had wanted to be, and what she is now forsaking, her eyes blurred into tears, and she, too, wept.

Jill explains why she has ''teacher burn-out'': ''I have to play so many different roles. I have to be the teacher, first and foremost, but I'm also the psychologist and the social worker and the nurse and the mother and the father and the janitor and . . . these children come to school upset because of broken homes. Some of their parents are alcoholics, drug addicts. They're in jail. And teachers are expected to deal with those problems so that the children can learn.

''I'm leaving because I'm not able to teach effectively and give the children quality education,'' she confessed. ''I just don't think the system works. And I am part of that system. I don't like being part of the system that doesn't work.''

''I have a first-grade level, a second-grade level, a third-grade level and a fourth-grade level and . . . It's difficult to teach four levels, especially when they are supposed to be learning fourth-grade skills and they are only reading on a first-grade level. I'd say I'm burned out. I feel that my teaching is a compromise. I feel the children are being cheated out of my good time, and out of my enthusiasm and out of my effort because of other things that I have to do.''

''But the main reason I'm leaving teaching is because I'm so frustrated and so stressed under all these circumstances and under these conditions.'' There remained, even in those last days, glimmers of that rare art she obviously owned: during recess, several students would approach her where she sitting alone at her desk, and hand her a book and then curl close to her as she would patiently read to them. She was that special being: a natural teacher. But she, and Rex Thomas, and countless others like them, will be lost to our nation's children, because we have asked of them so much—but given them so little.

One of Jill's students, John, a black child with large, grave, watchful eyes, was asked, ''What did you learn from Miss Baim?'' and he answered with a slow and thoughtful deliberation,

"How to—how to grow up and learn things. And how to do things when you're outside and you have a job. And raise a good family. And how to go on in life without quitting, and do things you've never done before. . . . She taught me how to be a man when I first came, came into the classroom. . . . I wish she'd stay here forever."

Another of her students, Veronicad, a Hispanic girl with long loose black hair framing an already beautiful face, offered, "She's a good teacher, and she teaches a lot, and—" She began crying, lifting an unsteady hand to cover her eyes, "—she's leaving."

She was told, "You'll have other teachers next year, you know."

Through her thick sobs, Veronicad blurted, "But she's a *good* teacher. . . ."

What is ultimately lost with the disappearance of teachers like Jill Baim, says Dr. Theodore Sizer, is "the opportunity for the youngsters that teacher would have known to be inspired, and hard learning follows inspiration. None of us works hard, uses our mind hard, without that kind of incentive. Every time you remove an inspiring teacher, you smother a spark."

Jill herself allowed, "I think they're losing a good teacher. But it's for my own happiness. I would not be happy in this situation anymore." And late one evening, in her apartment, she sat down at her typewriter and methodically tapped out her irrevocable letter of resignation—the aspiration of her girlhood ending in those measured hollow clacks.

Dr. Boyer observes, "In the end, this whole debate has to do with a teacher in the classroom. And I worry that while we're trying to improve the schools by legislative requirements and by national reports and by these experts on leave from Mount Olympus, we're going to forget that, in the end, good education means a good teacher."

Supervising teacher Tina Patterson was asked about the effect on children of having such a haphazard succession of teachers over a school year, and she answered with a rueful and pained helplessness, "How can anybody say that's educationally sound, for a child to spend a year that way? It would be foolish to say anything else. It's not educationally sound. We need more teachers. Unfortunately, the child suffers. That's unfortunately true—sad."

Children left without teachers. That is the final, poignant cost of the conditions now driving so many teachers from our classrooms. At Monroe High, the disillusionment had become terminal for Rex Thomas and some of his colleagues. Said one of them bitterly, "I'm not going to wait until I'm 65 and die with my boots on. I'm getting out of this. I don't get the response from those kids. I am fully frustrated with it, and from a financial standpoint, forget it. I loved teaching, and I loved it for many years, but you know, the last few years have been such frustration for me, I—I just can't tell you. I'm getting out."

The causes of this teaching crisis are bleakly clear: declining pay, declining respect, oppressive work conditions. In real dollars, teachers' salaries actually declined 12.2 percent while total personal income in the country went up almost 18 percent between 1972 and 1982. The median salary for an experienced teacher is half that of an experienced professional in private industry. The average starting salary ($12,769) is less than any other professional with similar education. And the gap relative to other professions widens the longer a teacher stays in. The average work week is 46.1 hours. It is slightly longer than the average blue collar work week; the pay is slightly less.

Over the last decade teachers have suffered a real *loss* in income of 13.7 percent—this, while personal income nationally, went *up* more than 17 percent. One of the teachers at Monroe High School laboring in his history class to break through student indifference is Rex Thomas, a truly inspirational teacher, who says: "I've always been taught that the value of anybody in society is the worth that they offer society. And then I laugh. Because if you look at the pay scale of people today who are pulling down enormous salaries and you ask yourself, what contribution they make to society, you find that rule is gone."

There has been a decline in status for the teacher. Years ago the teacher was the most educated and one of the most revered figures in the community. Now, in a society where everything is valued by the dollar, salary decline has hastened the decline of respect.

Salaries have always been low for teachers but they were offset by the inherent satisfaction of the work. Today, over a third of all teachers regard their job as an ordeal. A main reason: student behavior and attitudes toward learning. Few teachers entered the profession expecting that a large part of their time would be spent convincing students of the value of school, or cajoling them to work. But today, teachers teach in a more turbulent world, where students are less committed to school and less well-behaved, and where teachers have less power to do anything about it. Teachers can no longer assume that students come from stable homes, or that they will remain in the school system. Children from single parent homes are now the norm. They are more likely to get D's and F's, to be discipline problems, to drop out, to be absent, to bring alcohol and drugs into the classroom. For many of their students, there is no sense that school is worthwhile and, increasingly, teachers take that view of teaching, too. It seems simply too pointlessly exhausting. As one teacher put it, "Thirty of your thirty-five children would rather not be there."

In the middle of all this, teachers labor in a terrible isolation, helplessly caught in the oscillating policies of the educational establishment, not much more than functionaries obliged to carry out each new bureaucratic mandate. A continual landslide of state regulations—"remote-control education," as some experts style it—eventually engulfs even the most intrepid and resourceful teacher. These regulations, the increasing stress of "quantifiable performance" and test scores, debase the role of the teacher's individual art and judgment, reducing the teacher from a professional to a menial.

In the struggle to revive our public schools, the teacher must reach the student. But now teaching itself has become an imperiled profession because of increasingly oppressive conditions.

TO SAVE OUR SCHOOLS

As our public schools have widened their reach over the last decades, mounting responsibilities have fallen on teachers. Yet public respect for teaching has plunged and the salaries paid to teachers are the lowest of any comparably-educated profession. The toll of all this: the ever growing number of teachers who declare they would never choose teaching again. And the fact that the number of college students who would choose teaching today is less than at any time in the last thirty years.

And as more of the best and brightest desert the profession to which they felt called, the quality of those who remain, and of the dwindling numbers aspiring to enter, steadily deteriorates (for instance, in New York seven thousand teachers teach regularly without meeting the standards set by New York City and New York State)—posing the climactic peril to the state of teaching in the next decade. For the classrooms of this country, this means a grave shortage. And the peril is growing. A *general* shortage is feared by the end of this decade.

5. Distracted and Hostile Students

A major despair of teachers today is that many of the *students* they face daily are withdrawn into their teenage subculture, indifferent, detached from the classroom. Marty Sutherland, a teacher at Monroe High School, is an effusive young woman with a soft, blonde, frail comeliness about her, and an almost religious ardor for literature—which drew her into trying to teach it to others. What has kept her at it are rare moments of exhilaration at the sudden slow crackle of light in a student's eyes as an understanding begins to emerge. But what she has mostly encountered is a massive indifference of students now to precisely that experience of illumination. "This is a different generation that places education at the lowest priority," she said. "They come to school because there isn't anything better to do, or they come to school so they can make plans to do something else."

Confronting her are students whom she must pull through incredibly labored readings, one youth picking his way word by word through the sentence, *She was making sandwiches while Neil was pouring milk and Kevin was giving Stevie a piggyback ride.* . . . Another student replies to a question by muttering, "I wasn't paying any attention," and when Marty asks why, he merely snaps sullenly, "Because." Daily in her classroom, she battles to somehow connect these students to the larger life of books, ideas. "We have to really fight every single day to be legitimized to our student," she says, "That's dispiriting. We're up there saying, *Please look at me. I promise you it will be worth your while,* when we know that perhaps many of them feel, 'My God, I am wasting my time, I've got a hundred other things that I'd rather be doing.' One of five students chooses not to show up each day, and that's before the weather gets good."

Marty declares, "We are marooned in the classroom. The only real effective means that the teacher has is to somehow make his program saleable to a hostile audience. . . . And then here we go again. Teachers go back up there and they say, 'Look, give me another chance. This material that I'm going to teach you really counts.' " In the meantime, she takes refuge from the consistent disappointments of her classroom by retreating, each day after school, into an isolated private sanctuary at home among the small tropical birds she raises. "When I come home, I try very, very hard not to give any thought to how I spent my day. Raising little parrots is quite a pleasure to me. They're always there. They're glad to see me. And I don't get that during the day."

Asked, then, why she lingers on, why she continues trying, she begins, "It is a marvelous sensation—" and then her eyes glimmer with tears, her voice falters, "—to see students learning. And they just don't do it often enough. I *know* I know how to teach. I know that I can change someone's life if he'll just sit down and avail himself of it. I don't know of anything else that has given me that kind of satisfaction. I'm hoping that somehow, some way, parents will start to take a real involvement with their children, and that children will perceive the educational experience as a positive one. And, you know, give me a little more help. All I need is a little more help."

6. Lowered Public Esteem—Poor Pay

Commenting on the loss of esteem teachers face, Dr. Ravitch says: "The teacher has less respect than he or she would have had thirty or fifty years ago. At that time, there was almost an automatic respect for the teacher. The teacher was the most educated person in the community. That's no longer the case."

Indeed, the true worth of a teacher such as Rex Thomas can be seen in his inventive teaching—startling his class with his unsuspected lessons. Mr. Thomas has been teaching history and social studies at Monroe High, and other schools before it, for twenty-five years. He has been honored by Monroe as a master teacher, a model for student teachers. Soft-spoken and intense, with a frank open affable face under closely—barbered sandy hair, he is electric and inventive, in class with the gift of caring for a polymorphous variety of students. He personifies the best of the profession. But in recent years, he has only been able to confront another day in the classroom by jogging alone in the stillness of early mornings around a deserted race track near his house. Now, he is quitting it all. Rex Thomas has become another among the most sobering casualties of his profession. He admits he still can't envision himself doing anything else. But he is saying goodbye to it all with a cold anger: "I always enjoyed my classes that stirred me and disturbed me. . . . even to cast a doubt, gets something going in that student's mind . . . I cannot think of anything that would be more rewarding than teaching right now . . . You see it in a student's face and that's the reward you get. Or for a student to come up, say fifteen years later . . . I remember you, you're Mr. Thomas, aren't you? That . . . that touches me. I enjoy that."

The authentic worth of teachers, like Marty Sutherland and Rex Thomas can be divined in their inventive, alive teaching—galvanically expanding perceptions, perspectives, curiosities. One morning Rex Thomas startled his class with an unexpected lesson, beginning, "Okay, today what we're going to do is finish up on the idea of the credibility of witnesses. When

59

you get four people seeing the same action, many times you're going to get—'' At that point, a glowering youth came stalking into the room, and barked, ''I'd like to have a word with you.''

''What is it?'' said Thomas.

''This failure you gave me on my report card makes me ineligible for graduation, and I don't think it's really fair—'' At that, the youth swung and kicked at Thomas, who went to his knees between front rows of desks, calling out as the youth bolted from the room, ''Somebody get security. Somebody just go get security. Don't sit there. . . .'' He then got slowly back to his feet, brushing off his hands, gave a small smile, and said to the aghast and appalled gapes around him, ''All right, now let's see what we saw here,'' and as light hesitant laughs of realization spread around him, he wiped what seemed blood from his mouth and continued, ''Well, I have ketchup underneath here. All right, I want you to tell me what he said. Let's see if we make good witnesses.''

But the delights of teaching, for Rex Thomas, have been overcome by a sense of defeat. Approaching middle age, Thomas explains: ''If I were to start my life over again, as to a career, I certainly would not even consider teaching. It has deteriorated that much. One major obstacle is the fact that the salary isn't there as a motivational force. The other culprit is the enormous problems that teachers have to face that are not part of the educational program. It's such a watered-down version, that you often go home at night and wonder what the heck did I do today? Did I do any good today? Did I do any teaching, or was I just a clerk, filling in time and occupying space?''

This brief coda of one man's personal struggle against the dying of the light, clearly illustrates the perils within teaching. His is a struggle against all the adversaries of his profession and the forbidding realities of the larger society around him, to realize the democratic ideal of public education in an inner-city school of poor youths who, not that long ago in America, might have been discarded and lost, never dreaming of aspiring to anything more. His struggle is to bring to them now the fullest meaning of education—knowledge, understanding, light—so they may gain at least a chance of mastering their world, instead of being imprisoned by it.

And in his story, we are confronted with what we will all really lose if, because of disillusionment and despair, teachers like him are lost.

The principal frustration of the scanty pay is growing.

Indeed, over the last decade, teachers have suffered a real loss in income of 13.7 percent—while personal income nationally went up more than 17 percent. That both reflects and reinforces a corollary problem—the sinking respect, from students and society at large, in which teachers now toil. "Thirty or forty years ago," Dr. Ravitch observes, "there was almost an automatic respect for the teacher. . . . That's no longer the case. Teachers find themselves perhaps the lowest ranking of all professions. And find themselves struggling for the respect of the communities, struggling for the respect of parents, and struggling for the respect of their students.

I have asked some of my honors kids, kids who arc what I consider to be bright and hard-working, how many of them would go into the field of education," said Monroe High teacher, "and they laugh at me. When I ask them why, the answer is, 'Are you kidding? The kind of money you guys make?' " In his own class, Rex Thomas ventured, "How many students in here would think of taking up teaching as a career after they finish high school?" and contemplating the response, noted dryly, "We have one and a half. One or two." One student explained to him, "I got to say that I really respect teachers, what you guys do, but for my plans in life, I want to do something a little bit more money-making, I guess." Thomas himself confided, "The main reason why I'm considering retirement at an early age is the fact of the problems of finance. And we're having more difficulty now meeting our obligations than we did even five years ago."

7. The Places and the Players

In classrooms such as those in the Los Angeles school system and against the backdrop of the California State Los Angeles Teacher Training Institute, which supplies most of the teachers for those classrooms out of a reserve whose declining quality it largely perpetrates, we see the perils of the teaching profession sharply illuminated.

At Belmont High in Los Angeles, one principal has waged a private war against incompetence, a guerilla campaign to find and hold onto good teachers, to salvage the marginal, and to rout out the hopelessly inept—"the lemons," he calls them. John Howard is that principal, and he presides over the largest high school in California in a style that has earned him the aliases of "Patton" and "Caesar." Even so, Howard acknowledges the formidable rigors of trying to monitor 235 classrooms and he bristles over not being allowed to reward his best teachers—the teachers' union is bitterly opposed to such discrimination among teachers—and over being balked in getting rid of his worst ones. "How can I effectively manage a school without the authority to get rid of ineffective workers?" he demands.

In another Los Angeles school, that frustration has so exasperated its principal that he chooses to discuss with us the problem of one incompetent teacher—though not by name. The principal declares it will take at least two years to finally extricate the teacher from school—if, in fact, he can bring it off—and in the meantime, that teacher will continue to "simply waste the lives" of the children in his classes.

Another instance of the struggle within the teaching profession is the angry resistance of teachers' unions to increasingly popular proposals for reforming the state of teaching. Their resistance could act to confound real teaching reform. It could also subvert the essential effort to reclaim community faith in the public school system.

With the surge of national misgivings about our schools, and the teachers in them, governors and state authorities have reacted with massive programs to overhaul their public school systems. Many of those programs have begun by focusing on the teachers themselves.

But across the country, many suggestions are meeting with passionate resistance from the powerful National Education Association which bills them as discriminatory, humiliating, scapegoating, token, and backward. With their energetic attention to the needs of belabored teachers, the NEA and its rival union, the American Federation of Teachers, together with other smaller unions, have won the loyalty of some 86 percent of our entire teaching corps over the last few decades. This makes teaching the most thoroughly unionized profession in the nation.

It's not hard to understand why. Isolated in their schools, isolated in society, laboring under conditions and for wages that have reduced them to little more than white-collar mill hands, teachers have found the union the one sole strength and hope they have. That massive and fervent loyalty has, in turn, given the NEA and AFT extraordinary power in virtually every dispute where teachers detect a threat to their position. And neither union has been shy about asserting that power.

At the same time, though, profoundly protective of the gains they've won for their teachers, both unions have proven reluctant, defensive, sluggish about strenuously policing the competency of those within their memberships. As a result, they are now confronted with the likelihood that local legislators and boards of education, responding to a popular outcry for "teacher accountability," will begin policing those teachers for them. Battles are thus building over the country.

In state after state, legislation is gathering to install merit pay for the excellent, and competency tests to filter out the unfit. And even though the NEA and AFT are now grudgingly accepting some of those measures, they view them as simplistic and myopic quick fixes which are oblivious to the far more fundamental and wholesale extensions of energy and money it will take to revive the school system.

And in state after state, these looming confrontations could lead to stand-offs balking any real movement toward reform; they could even accelerate the decline of our teaching force into the 1990's. Recent reform battles in several states have already demonstrated the power of the unions and still more of them are coming up against union opposition. Since most teachers in the public schools work under union-negotiated labor contracts, many crucial educational reforms fall subject to contractual negotiation. For example, states and localities probably could not enact reforms in the following areas without undertaking bargaining with the teachers' unions—which would also be delayed until a contract is up for renewal: changes in length of the school day or year, merit pay, dismissal of incompetent teachers, requirements for assigning and grading of homework, allowing non-teacher-certified professionals to teach part-time (such as mathematicians and scientists), requirements for in-service training of teachers, teacher lay-offs based on need and talent rather than seniority. The intrusion of teacher unionism into the reform process is such that one expert has asserted "public sector bargaining poses insuperable obstacles to the educational reform movement."

On no front has that confrontation emerged more clearly than in Arkansas. Its vigorous and affable young governor, Bill Clinton, has made school reform his central campaign theme in his quest for reelection this November. Last fall, he got through the legislature a comprehensive education bill, including a pay raise for teachers, with a one percent increase of the sales tax to finance it—no small achievement in a poor, rural state which last allowed a sales tax hike some twenty-six years ago. But the worm in the apple, according to many Arkansas teachers, is a stipulation that all of them, new and veteran alike, must pass a basic literacy test by at least 1987 to keep their certification.

Clinton insists he could not have passed his reform program, and the tax increase to fund it, without that teacher accountability measure—and polls like the 16th Annual Gallup poll of the Public's Attitudes Toward Schools do indicate a wide popular will for it. Nevertheless, the NEA-affiliated teachers' union in Arkansas, one of the most formidable features on the political landscape, has mobilized against the reform program and against Bill Clinton. To do so, it has enlisted at least one impressive ally: the Educational Testing Service in Princeton, author of the SAT's, which has refused Arkansas the use of its teacher examination to carry out Clinton's plan.

An unhappy irony is, while Bill Clinton may be an ambitious young politician, the renaissance of Arkansas's schools seems a genuine passion with him. Still, Arkansas teacher unions regard his test as insulting, a political stunt, they call it, they find it utterly superficial compared to what's really needed—a reliable procedure of simple teacher evaluation. But Clinton is refusing to relent, contending that the test is a proper answer to deep public concerns, and that it is only the beginning of a much larger reform effort anyway.

And, indeed, there are teachers scattered across Arkansas who support Clinton, with whatever mixed feelings, and have declared they will take the test. At Central High in Little Rock, sixty-eight teachers have defected from their union's position, describing it as a political blunder that could further sabotage the image of Arkansas teachers, and they have signed a petition to consent to the test, if that is what's required to restore public confidence in the schools. But for the most part, Arkansas teachers are outraged. Many vow they will quit their classrooms before submitting to the test. Even though Clinton has presented the test as an unavoidable condition for getting the tax hike which will raise their salaries, these teachers assert it will only lift them to forty-ninth in the country's scale of teacher pay.

The collision in Arkansas between a governor and a teachers' union has launched us into a wider examination of the role of teachers' unions in America's prospects for regenerating its schools—how strikes and union demands, and the general opposition to merit pay and accountability tests have tended to affect the image of teachers in this country, and how *that* may affect the quality of teachers we can expect over the next decade.

The toughest conclusions reached by the most distinguished authorities say that it is necessary for teachers to be held accountable for high standards of teaching, whether those standards are set by the teachers themselves, or by the state. But they also argue that the public must make high standards of teaching *possible*, by supporting teachers, paying them sufficiently so that it will be an attractive profession, able to draw the most gifted and committed students to it. They ask, finally, what good are competency tests if the profession becomes so substandard that no applicant can pass them, and there is no one waiting to replace those driven out of the profession?

The real challenge of the future is not how to get rid of incompetent teachers—a minimum action at best—but how to reinvigorate and give new life to a profession which is central not only to the future of the nation's children, but to the strength of its leadership.

Beyond Bill Clinton, the teachers and union officials, are some further—and central—players. Walter and Marylou Smiley are parents of two children in the public schools of Little Rock. Their son Vance has had two bad teachers in a row. Their daughter has had one of these teachers and will get the other next year. Vance's test scores have been dropping for two years and the Smileys are worried he'll be placed in a slow track in junior high and after that in high school. Walter Smiley has taken to documenting the evidence of the teachers' incompetence, hoping to convince somebody to do something. The principal of his children's school is trying to help, but getting rid of a teacher isn't easy. Mr. Smiley says he wanted to sue somebody, but the system is so complex and diffuse he can't figure out whom to sue.

Like many parents, the Smileys are confused about what to do. They never thought that as parents they would have to ferret out and document incompetent teachers. They consider the literacy test as an enheartening first step, though hardly the solution. Their son's teacher, they suspect, will probably pass such a paper quiz. Something more fundamental is clearly needed to renew the teaching profession. The question for the Smiley's, and families like them over the country, is whether the current alarm will translate into the sustained exertion and financial commitment essential to effect a real reformation in teaching, and whether that possibility will be facilitated or blindly sabotaged by teachers' unions.

The more fundamental problems are not indigenous to one school but are enlarging phenomena, spreading across the nation.

8. The Rising Mediocrity

Who will replace the Rex Thomases, the Jill Baims, in the schools of America?

With the oppressive conditions in the classroom—and with more lucrative professional opportunities now open to women and minorities—there has developed a massive migration of talent out of teaching. It's already clear that at least half of our teaching force will have to be replaced over the next decade. That prospect is an unsettling one. Because what shadows the future of our schools even more than the exodus of veteran teachers, is the uncertain quality of those emerging to succeed them. Those now being drawn into teaching are coming from the lower reaches of the academic spectrum.

The SAT scores of prospective teachers have dropped *80 points* below the average for high school seniors, lower than any group except those going into vocational training, ethnic studies, or home economics. In the last ten years, the SAT verbal scores for education majors dropped 27 points, more than the decline in the national average. SAT math scores for aspiring teachers dropped 31 points, *twice* the decline in the national average.

The combination of circumstances now at work will only hasten that slide of quality unless some way is found to radically overhaul the conditions of teaching, and to arrest the flight of the finest. Otherwise, we face a long twilight of excellence in the teaching profession—a drift toward mediocrity that could blight the profession for years to come, and so endanger the very life-nerve of our public schools.

To begin with, the nation's schools of education, which prime and prepare teachers for our classrooms, are themselves becoming academic barrens. With their enrollment having fallen by half over the last ten years, the students left to them hardly represent a survival of the fittest. Faced with a dwindling reserve of applicants, many schools of education have simply relaxed their standards to maintain a level of enrollment that will protect their budgets. Stiffer requirements would likely put a number of ed-

68

ucation departments, already scrabbling to survive, out of business altogether. Indeed, some of the better colleges and universities already have eliminated teacher training because of the shortage of applicants.

Some results of the slackening of standards in California: a *third* of the teacher candidates emerging from education schools there fail a state-required test of basic reading, writing, math skills. At the school of education at Cal State L.A., one of the largest in California, potential teachers must take a basic skills test to be admitted. The surreal irony is, they need not pass the test—merely take it. As it happens, a sizeable portion flunk it.

The education program at Cal State was described by one student, Sharrin Heinrich, as "Push people in, get 'em out, churn 'em out. "Right now, teachers are needed, so I think they're trying to get as many into the program without examining the program first. Get 'em in and get 'em out." Sharrin, herself an "A" student, confided, "I can get by with very little studying. To be honest, some classes, I never cracked a book, and I was still able to pull 'A's."

Another Cal State student, Michael Dean, assessed the caliber of most others in the education program as "bottom of the barrel. You get what you pay for. I mean, it's no mystery. They're paying the lowest to be a teacher. People with good intellects, good communications skills, are going into something else."

But California is hardly alone in turning out legions of inadequate teaching prospects. In Houston, Texas, more than 40 percent of new teachers failed a basic skills test. In Montgomery County, Maryland, 45 percent of English teacher applicants failed an English test. And in Florida, 10 percent of teacher education programs were closed down because of high failure rates on a state-required test.

In short, says Professor Michael Kirst, of Stanford University, "In many institutions, it's virtually open enrollment to get into teaching—they'll take almost anybody."

One bleak consequence of all this: dim teachers tend to reproduce themselves in dim students—from whom, in turn, the next generation of teachers will be emerging.

TO SAVE OUR SCHOOLS

Once teachers graduate from education schools and pass on into the classroom, they find themselves caught in a vast, labyrnthine system oblivious to their individual strengths or needs, with little hope for increased pay or responsibilities beyond the factor, as one chancellor put it, of having "breathed longer in the classroom." There are only the most scanty and desultory procedures for evaluating teachers' performances—for rewarding the best, filtering out the clearly unfit, or, perhaps most important, for aiding those teachers who might be salvageable. Monroe High's Marty Sutherland reported, "The evaluation process is currently—well, it's a farce. We are evaluated by an administrator who spends, at most, two fifty-minute periods in our classroom every two years. This is not quality control."

At the same time, there's little to encourage the more capable teachers to exert themselves to teach at their best. Teachers' unions although now reexamining the concepts, have long and vigorously resisted pay raises based on judgments of merit, terming such a system "discriminatory." The result is a kind of professional void, with little accountability, little impetus toward excellence. While this acts to steadily impoverish the profession of its most able, the middling or outright incompetent teachers cling on, and proportionately expand.

Distinguished Professor Chester Finn, of Vanderbilt University, laments, "There's no reward for becoming a better teacher, because we don't do anything for better teachers. There is no punishment for becoming a worse teacher, because we don't do anything about incompetent teachers. So it simply exhausts any sense of quality from the system."

What overshadows the future of our schools even more than the exodus of veteran teachers is the fact that we are drawing our future teachers from the lower reaches of the academic spectrum. With more professional opportunities now open to women and minorities, there has been a massive migration of talent out of teaching.

Over the next decade, because of teachers leaving and retiring from the profession, we will have to replace at least half of our teaching force. That simple fact is ominous because if we don't act now to make teaching more attractive to the talented the quality of our next generation of teachers, by all the evidence, will seriously decline. What that bodes is a twilight of excellence in the teaching profession—a drift toward mediocrity endangering the profession for years to come and, ultimately, the very nerves and life of our public schools.

Schools of education which prepare teachers for our classrooms are in danger of becoming academic wastelands. Not only are those aspiring to teach less academically able, but there are fewer and fewer of them. Enrollment has fallen by half over the last ten years and although some schools of education are now raising standards, many have simply lowered them to keep their programs populated, their budgets secure. One result, in California: a *third* of the teacher candidates emerging from schools of education failed a required test of basic reading, writing and math skills.

As one spokesman said: "I think it's very damaging to an occupation that's centrally concerned with learning and the life of the mind to have people who are not academically capable, let alone distinguished, going into such a profession."

The final casualties of the decay in America's teaching corps are the children—their future more limited, possibilities denied them. Once teachers pass into the classroom they find themselves caught in a system moving inevitably toward mediocrity. The evaluation of teachers is uneven and the principals who evaluate are often poorly qualified. Study after study has found our present forms of evaluation almost meaningless for guaranteeing the quality of teaching. As yet there is no simple, timely procedure for filtering out the clearly unfit, and there is no incentive to excel: teachers' unions have long opposed pay raises based on merit. The result is a professional void, with little accountability, little impetus toward excellence.

There are few statistics on teacher incompetence—but *one* which is available, is startling: When over eleven thousand *vet-*

71

eran teachers volunteered to take the California teacher test, *one third* of them failed it. School principals say from 5 to 15 percent of their teachers are inadequate. Most resort to informal pressures to force those teachers out. Few school systems are willing to undergo the long and costly legal struggle to dismiss clearly bad teachers, protected by tenure laws. In the last forty-three years, only eighty-six tenured teachers have been formally dismissed for incompetency . . . in the entire nation.

Problem teachers in Los Angeles are usually moved to another school for a second chance, and then maybe to a third, before dismissal proceedings are even begun. In the meantime, they are still teaching children. The process appalls some principals. Robert McLachlan, the principal at Parmalee Elementary School, explains his and our problem: "We have outstanding teachers . . . then, on the other hand, we have teachers who have passed the exams and have been assigned who should not be anywhere near a classroom . . . I have one teacher whose class I've been in twenty-five times; I have not seen anything but mathematics, and I've been in there at all different hours. This is horrendous; to me it says those children probably will not learn to read. Children who have been in that class, their scores have gone down radically. The child, the class that this teacher had last year, the children scored, as an example, in vocabulary in the sixty-sixth percentile. The year before, that same child scored in the ninetieth percentile. This teacher should not be allowed to be in a classroom anywhere. And the sad thing about the whole thing, even though I would issue an unsatisfactory, which I intend to do, in all likelihood, that teacher will be transferred to another school. Which means another group of thirty children will waste another year. We have a contract that supports incompetent teachers, and it's a pity.

However, Judy Solokovits, the Los Angeles teachers union head, crisply defends the legal complications necessary to fire teachers: "The tenure law is not too protracted at all and due process is not too protracted when you are now saying that someone who has been judged as being qualified and competent, has now . . . an issue has been raised as to their competency. They deserve every protection that can possibly be given to them.''

But for the vast majority of teachers, the problem is not incompetency, but a losing battle against daunting odds. Most teachers are isolated in their classrooms with little guidance or support, left to face mounting adversities on their own. As Dr. David Berliner Professor of Educational Psychology at the university of Arizona noted: "I think the number of very bad teachers is very small. I think the number of teachers who could use improvement is very large." That's really the failure, I think, in American education today . . . we've stopped providing feedback to those people after they're on the job. The damage for people who aren't getting any help is that they continue their bad habits, and they burn out. They know they're not effective, and they wonder why, and over time, they forget to care. And they went into teaching because they *did* care. People go into teaching, certainly not for the money, certainly not for the prestige—they go in because they have a calling. . . . They need to be rejuvenated. They need to feel competent and effective again.''

There are teacher centers around the country where teachers help teachers to renew their craft. But their numbers are small, and the need is overwhelming. Because if teaching is left in its limbo of isolation and mediocrity, it will imperil our hopes for our schools, our dreams for our children. Nancy Larson works at one such center in Rowland, near Los Angeles. "Ours is a very hands-on kind of program, where, first of all, we bring in live kids, and do demonstration lessons ourselves. I think the fact that we are all classroom teachers really adds to our credibility.''

Since the program at Rowland began, student test scores in the district moved up steadily. Testifies one teacher re-trained at the center, "It focuses and forces you to become a good teacher. . . . It is trying to bring back pride and dignity to the teaching profession." And Nancy Larson observes, "We've kind of been beaten down as a trade. But I think things like this program, where teachers get a sense of their skill—perhaps they won't feel so helpless, and won't be leaving in droves, as they are. It may just be one very small light. But I think we've got to try anything we can.''

But programs like that at Rowland to redeem marginal teachers are still rare over the country, and exist tenously from year to year on uncertain funding and grants. The need for them, however, is massive and strategic. Because if teaching is left to languish in its limbo now of disregard and mediocrity, it will centrally sabotage our hopes for our schools, our dreams for our children. The final casualties of the decay in America's teaching corps are America's children—their future more limited, possibilities denied them, their world inevitably more meager and cramped.

One crucible where that conflict is being played out most hotly is the state of Arkansas. In 1957, this community flared into the national attention. Federal troops were ordered in to enforce the integration of Central High School, Little Rock, Arkansas. In 1984 once again, Arkansas was the stage for a bitter confrontation over schools . . . that carries national repercussions. Arkansas has become the first state to require veteran teachers to pass a literacy test or lose their license to teach. The proposal has met with a storm of teacher opposition. One explained her vehement opposition: ''I will not take this test! I will quit!''

Another said: ''I love my job; I love my profession, but I will not tolerate this any more!''

The battle between public officials and teachers intensifies over the larger question of teaching reform. On one side: state legislatures and governors, moving to fill the vacuum of leadership in assessing teacher quality, insisting on new accountability measures. Eighteen states have already instituted entry tests to measure teacher competency. Nineteen are proposing career ladder programs like merit pay to reward and keep the best teachers, but many teachers oppose this measure.

At risk here is whether the clash, between politicians demanding stricter measurements of teacher quality, and teachers' unions resisting their proposals, will so reduce and embitter the issue that the nation will lose sight of the need for more difficult, but more fundamental reforms.

The politician may be in danger of advertising quick fixes. And some unions may have entered into a disastrous political myopia in resisting popular reforms like competency testing and merit pay—eroding public willingness to address the larger imperatives for reform.

Seventy-eight percent of teachers of the 86 percent sympathetic to union goals have now joined them—making teaching one of the most unionized fields in America. The unions have fought hard for traditional labor concerns like salary and job security. Obligated as labor unions to defend their members from dismissal, they've often been reluctant to police their quality in general. That means, a recent major study concluded: "The unions . . . have protected their weakest members rather than winning rewards for their strongest . . . The result is that the quality of teaching suffers . . ."

Hope for the renewal of American education finally lies in reversing the decay of teaching, restoring it to a noble profession. And like all the other hopes for saving our public schools, this struggle too must begin, not only at a national level, but in each of this nation's sixteen thousand school systems, those states and cities and communities across the country—communities like yours.

The drift toward mediocrity and outright incompetence, that threatens the teaching profession's future is already evident.

Dr. Ernest Boyer, asked if teaching had become an imperiled profession, reflected, "Yes, I think I'd choose that word. Can this nation start to give additional status to the teacher and honor and reward those who are truly outstanding, and cause teachers to feel more— and I choose this term carefully—more *empowered?* Instead of at the bottom of the totem pole, help them feel that they're at the heart of the enterprise. If we don't rekindle some fire around that vision, we're going to go through this period with more regulations and requirements and schools that are less vital than when the debate began."

Dr. Ravitch says: "When we talk about improving the teaching profession, I keep coming back to the need for teachers to have some control over their own work lives. To have some professional involvement in the decisions that are made about curriculum, about teaching style, about the evaluation of other teachers, of new teachers.''

Michael Kirst of Stanford warns, ''If you're going to improve the teaching profession, we're going to have to move on all fronts simultaneously. You have to move on recruitment, on teacher training, on the in-service training of teachers, the job conditions. It's going to take a whole series of events, and interventions, moving simultaneously.''

Dr. Ravitch proposes, ''In the first instance, there should be an entry level test for teachers. It's not insulting. It's not insulting to a lawyer or a doctor to take a medical board exam, or a bar exam. Entry into a profession should be accompanied by an examination.'' Dr. Boyer would expand the evaluation process: ''Teacher evaluation at the point of entrance and teacher evaluation at the point of tenure. And I frankly believe there should be continuing teacher evaluation periodically throughout one's career.''

Beyond that, says Dr. Ravitch, ''What the profession needs today is something that's been called a career ladder. Tennessee has a structure now where you enter at one level of teaching as a kind of novice teacher, an apprentice teacher. You go on to become a kind of an assistant teacher, and you work your way up to being a master teacher. The master teachers are paid much more than the novice teachers—so that one can aspire as a professional.''

This complex endeavor would demand more, of course, than simple infusions of money, but any genuine revitalization of teaching would be impossible without that, and enormously expensive. Simply to bring the profession more into line with salary levels in comparable professions would require about a 25 percent pay increase for all teachers, at a cost, it's been estimated, of some 15 billion dollars.

But the renewal of America's public schools—and all that's at stake in that for America's own future—finally lies in rescuing the teaching profession, restoring it to its traditional high place in the life of our society. The question is whether the current alarm about our schools will translate into the sustained exertion and financial commitment essential to bring that about—to effect a real reformation in teaching. At the heart of that challenge, as we have seen in Arkansas, is really a larger exertion to win back the community faith vital to save our public schools, and their unfulfilled promise, from the impending dangers of the next decade.

PART III

The Perilous Decade:
PUBLIC FAITH

9. Desertion by the Middle Class

The final great threat to public education in the next decade is the danger that the vast middle class of this country—will abandon the public school system—depriving the schools of the vital leadership and support they so desperately need.

In the words of John Goodlad, "The high schools of this nation are only as strong as the communities of which they are a part." With less money available from federal, state and local governments, schools are increasingly forced to rely on the citizens of their own communities—their time, their money, their effort. But sinking test scores, undisciplined classes, inadequate school facilities—and memories of turmoil from the recent huge effort to more widely democratize our public schools, along with deep and abiding racial and class prejudices—have set off an exodus from the public schools. And those leaving are the very people whose support and political leadership are most crucial to the survival of public education.

Another of the major problems within the American educational system which has caused a further erosion of public faith is the perceived bureaucracy. The public has become aware that of the $7 billion of federal funds budgeted for state and local education in the early nineteen eighties, over $916.5 million was used for personnel expenses. Four million people are employed by the public elementary and high schools in the United States but only a little over half of these are teachers! Taxpayers cannot help but shake their heads in wonder at the number of coordinators, assistants, liaison officers, research personnel, clerical and secretarial staff as well as cooks, dieticians, dishwashers and the non-professional staff on school payrolls.

To concerned taxpayers surveying their property tax bills, the largest item is local taxes for education. Even though enrollment in schools has declined since the peak year of 1971, the cost of public elementary and secondary education has continued to rise. Thus, the public judges that too much money is being wasted. There is little doubt that many bureaucratic expenditures are justifiable. However, there is also little doubt that there are some overlapping functions, layers of position titles within the same area, irregularities in office expenditures at educational headquarters, overabundant staff members and special bureaus or divisions for programs which could be supervised by already existing agencies.

The nation is experiencing a fiscal crunch and education must come to grips with its effects. In order to reduce the administrative costs of education beneath the 13 percent at which it currently operates, some jobs and programs have to be cut. Yet, if money is to be spent on new important efforts to improve existing educational systems, productive trimming and the reordering of priorities must occur. Naturally, the bureaucracy of large districts is more extensive and costly than in small districts; however, even in very small school systems there must be close scrutinizing of the number of people on the school payroll who are not directly connected to the classrooms. One of the proposals to correct overabundant administrative personnel is to consolidate districts or to form cooperative arrangements with communities nearby. Unfortunately, such arrangements would interfere with the desire to preserve local control of schools and that is another problem with which to be dealt.

However, the disillusionment of those who must vote for and ultimately pay for our schools must be considered. And the message they are sending to those concerned with reforming education is loud and as yet unheeded. This message is "school, heal thyself" before dispatching further pleas for more funding. Those in control of today's educational system must take a long critical look at the economics of current budgets, a survey of non-professional and professional employees, a reevaluation of the existing bureaucracy. Then a productive pruning must be instituted, because only when the public sees inner reform will the schools get the support from the community they so badly need.

If the public school system cannot regain the faith of these middle Americans within the next few years, the country's educational system could split into two separate and starkly unequal school systems, a division which has already begun—a healthy suburban system, mostly white and comfortable on the one side; a huge custodial system in the inner cities for the growing population of the poor and non-white on the other—this fissure will deepen, and become a permanent, irrevocable part of the American landscape.

To say that the American public today is fully committed to an anti-public education posture is as inaccurate and as dangerous as saying that public education and its leadership can do no wrong, that the public will stand for anything.

Still, the fact must be faced that even where a legitimate and long-standing marriage has existed between public education and its public, misunderstandings have emerged and divorce may be contemplated. Some of the problems ravaging the public schools today are, at their core, problems of public relations: missed signals, poor planning, muddled thinking and, sadly, inept or possibly ill-trained leadership. These problems are, for the most part, both predictable and preventable. Where they occur, they do so because education managers—boards, superintendents, principals, even leaders of teacher unions and parent groups—have either lost or never developed the sense of place, purpose, and perspective which the public at large expects.

Many of these management errors bring immediate, negative results. Of even greater concern, however, is the "mind set" which leads to a repetition of such errors, particularly those with delayed but devastating effects.

These reasons have caused one of the first warning signals of loss of faith in the public school system, American tax payers' reluctance to fund it. At a time of expanding school costs and contracting school budgets, the elemental question arises: who is going to pay the cost of saving our public school system?

There is national recognition that our schools are in trouble. According to polls, reforming our school system is a growing concern rivaled only by national security. But the reforms urged in the report, "A Nation at Risk," would require an additional $14 billion. And so far, neither the President nor the public has shown any readiness to supply funds of that magnitude. President Reagan, while calling for more rigorous schooling, has not only frozen federal educational funds at a level lagging behind the climbing inflation rate, but has actually moved to reduce the federal budget for education.

While the per capita cost of education *is* high, the children most costly to educate are those of the poor and disadvantaged, those whose homes are often broken and whose parents, usually undereducated themselves, are least able to provide increased school support. Yet there seems, so far, little realization that while the price of literacy in America may be high, the price of illiteracy is higher still.

The public is aware that the inner-city schools in 1984 were trapped in a climate of violence, racism and apathy. These city schools have fallen victim to the community's loss of faith. They now struggle isolated, on their own. While the President, the state, the city are appealing for schools like these to turn themselves around, no one's offering the money with which to do it.

Theodore Sizer, Chairman of the Education Department at Brown University asks: "How do you turn around the quality of a school where the teachers face 180 kids a day, where the truancy levels are 50 percent and you don't even have the people to go out and find the youngsters? Where the youngsters have no hot

meals unless they're delivered to that school . . . How do you look the principal of that high school . . . a high school with those conditions . . . in the eye and say, 'Oh, you know, we're not going to add any more money, turn it around by the force of your personality?' That's unrealistic.''

Heroic teachers in inner-city schools battle on as funds dwindle. Impoverished schooling threatens to lock these students outside the main life and promise of America. In inner cities, hundreds of thousands of children who came into the system educationally at risk, now attend educationally-deprived schools. At Central High in Kansas, many academic classes have been dropped, limiting even the most ambitious students. The decay of such schools as Central High, has followed the steady decline in support for urban schools that began in the 1970's.

In 1984, Bruce Bailey was a senior there, a 17-year-old with a 3.5 grade average. Long, languid, loping, hugely likable, he was one of the top high school basketball players in the state and has won an athletic scholarship to Colorado State University. But, as he prepared to move into that seemingly more promising future, he was deeply uneasy that he has already been betrayed by his schooling in Central, that his future has already been maimed, if not aborted. Watching Bailey browsing over a crossword test on insurance in a "Home Ec" class, one gets a chilling sense that his fear could be well-founded. He explains, "I feel like I've lost something . . . You know, I've left something behind, or I've missed a couple of steps. You know. I know that I can handle and challenge anyone, you know, to a certain extent, but then I think, I say, hey, well . . . the students, the teaching . . . I'm not striving, or I'm not being pushed . . . this is not being put on my mind or anything. And I feel like, you know, they are a couple of steps ahead of me and I do worry about this sometimes.''

City schools like this one are now imperiled by federal cutbacks, inadequate state budgets, community indifference. Wealthier suburban school systems are still holding their own, but the growing number of taxpayers who are childless and aging and therefore without direct concern, threatens them, too.

The question echoes: Who will pay the cost of saving our public school system?

After a decade of resistance, some local communities are proposing increasing their school allocation budgets, some states are moving to increase legislative support. From middle America to the wealthiest suburbs to the inner city, there is now real concern over money for schools. Federal funds for the disadvantaged in the poorest districts have been cut. While there have always been sharp differences between school systems, the federal cutbacks and a tightened economy have deepened the divisions between urban and suburban schools: between poor districts in central cities with little taxpayer support and the stronger systems on the outskirt of the cities . . . another America.

For instance, Anne Wooster's parents moved across the state line to the Shawnee Mission School district in Kansas because of the extraordinary quality of the public schools. She says: "I think I've gotten probably the best college preparation . . . education that I could have gotten, maybe even in a private institution. I've been very happy in public school." The community of Shawnee demands excellent schools and can afford them. Here, in the past fifteen years, every school tax referendum but one has been passed. Across the line in the Kansas City, Missouri, district, every school tax proposal but one has been rejected in the past fifteen years.

In Shawnee, as in the best public school systems across the country, education is a community faith. Shawnee boasts a high number of honor students, national merit scholars, Westinghouse Science winners, Presidential scholars.

At that school in the summer of 1983, Anne Wooster greeted a distinguished visitor. His visit was part of a major new presidential crusade: Ronald Reagan spoke of the report to the Commission on Excellence in Education, "A Nation At Risk":

"The Commission recommends . . . four years of English, three years of mathematics . . . three years of science, three years of social studies, and a half-a-year of computer science. History shows that during the time when America built the greatest system of education the world has ever seen—and it is still a great system—the work, the planning and the money were all supplied by states and local school districts with no federal interference.''

10. Decreased Financial Support

Since 1981, as a result of reduced federal funds, almost a million students—those generally most critically in need in our schools—have been dropped from federal support services such as remedial classes. At the same time, state governments have produced a flurry of alarming reports and legislative mandates for reform which most of them then balk at financing.

At the local level, those disenchanted with public schools have repeatedly rejected school bond issues or tax levies designed to assist struggling school systems. What's more, with a falling birth rate and aging population, a growing number of Americans have no direct investment in the schools in their communities and minimal enthusiasm for new taxes to support them.

So, faced with growing deficits and expenses, more and more schools have had to turn to special private sources. A measure of this new dependency is that, in 1983, according to the annual report of the American Association of Fund-Raising Counsel Inc., 9.04 billion dollars was raised from individual Parent-Teacher Associations, corporate donors, bequests and foundations. But while business interests are recognizing the link between a healthy school system and a healthy working force, their contributions tend to be directed toward the more affluent suburban schools, where the white middle class is dominant and school taxes already substantial.

Within our cities, however, the funding shortfall is reaching a state of crisis that threatens to become even more critical over the next decade. Such school districts now find themselves caught in a grim and deepening impasse. Left much more dependent on citizen support through taxes or voluntary aid, they are without the resources to rehabilitate their schools into the successes that would then, in turn, attract that desperately needed support.

In the Kansas City, Missouri, school district, for example, almost 65 percent of the budget is raised from local sources. The life or death of the central city schools hangs, in a large measure, on community support. Yet, since 1967, almost every attempt to raise school financing has been defeated. While there's wide awareness that the school district is desperate for funds, fundamental disaffection, indifference, and racial suspicions have confounded most efforts for financial rescue of Kansas City's schools.

And Kansas City's situation is not unique. As the number of disadvantaged children in the schools continues to mount and the district budgets continue to dwindle, the consequences for the disadvantaged children of the inner city are cruelly clear: overloaded classrooms, reduction of academic courses, inadequate textbooks, fewer and less capable remedial teachers, decimation of counseling staffs, aging school buildings that are taking on the look of the slums around them—all serving to accelerate the flight of students from more ambitious middle-class homes, black and white, to the reassurances of the suburbs. The continuing hemorrhage of these students out of Kansas City's system not only depletes the morale and energy in the schools they've abandoned, but, in reducing the local tax base, makes it yet more difficult for this inner-city system to find the funding support it needs.

Across the state line, where Anne Wooster now goes to school in Kansas, is Kansas City's mirror image. Shawnee is affluent, a prosperous community of pleasant lawns and substantial homes, which supports its school district with a galaxy of resources and programs that makes the Kansas City system resemble one in a Third World country. In Shawnee, judicious investments of savings produce more income than federal grants. Yet in Shawnee, too, there is an unease about the tightening economy which is reflected by a spirited public relations campaign to insure community commitment to its schools. Ten years ago, 70 percent of the households in Shawnee Mission had children in school. Today, in a reversal, 70 percent do not. The superintendent recognizes that the continuing health of his schools rests on involving those who sooner or later will be voting on his financial needs, a populace not intimately connected to the children within the system.

For both Shawnee and the Missouri inner city, the survival and strength of their schools will be a measure of the interest of the communities around them. But after all the federal reports and speeches, the schools find themselves left to their own devices; they face the formidable task of galvanizing their own communities into providing concern and money enough to secure their future.

If America's public schools are to be saved, then, it's a struggle that will be won or lost on the local community level.

As we've mentioned, Kansas City has, rather than the indistinguishable mirror-towered Everycity look of so much of metropolitan America in the Eighties, still an archaic mellowness of how Middle American cities used to look in the Fifties—and the schools on the Missouri side reflect that same look: those musty brick citadels of dimly gleaming corridors which most of us remember from our own childhoods, constructed in what had to have been an extraordinary burst of public school construction all across the country in the Thirties.

At the same time, though, Kansas City is an image of the developing schisms threatening the public school systems of so many cities today. And it's here that we will examine, directly and intimately, the actual evolution of that threat, as well as its potentially tragic costs to the children of both the dispossessed and the privileged—and the enormous odds against which a few alarmed citizens and parents in Kansas City, Missouri, are battling somehow to restore the credibility of their public schools. What is at stake here, in their own uncertain struggle, is surely by projection, at stake for the entire country.

President Reagan's speech entitled: "Excellence and Opportunity: A Program of Support For American Education" warned of a rising tide of mediocrity and recommended an immediate raising of standards. It is estimated that the recommendations would cost $14 billion to accomplish, but the President made it plain that reform should be financed by states and local communities. In Shawnee, where scholastic standards had been raised without presidential urging or federal funds, the President's hard line about money went all but unnoticed.

But in Kansas City, Missouri—where reform was desperately needed—the message was painful. A music teacher summed up the desperate plight of many: "I was allocated for band and choir sixty-five dollars for the year . . . for music. One band number can cost fifty-five dollars. I think that says it all . . . A lot of times I spend money out of my own pocket to get these kids the music that they need. They wrote us a letter and told us that the money has run out. So we do the best we can with what we have . . ."

In one remedial high school class, the youngsters are reading at a third, fourth and fifth grade level. Their teacher has had only two weeks special training. The district can no longer afford specialists to work with teenagers who barely read or write. Since the mid-1960's, early remedial classes with specially-trained teachers had been funded by the federal government. Now these funds have dried up.

The desegregation suit in Kansas City was brought in the name of retiring school board president, Joyce Stark's two children. Stark now says, "There are only three or four major institutions that the public has ongoing responsibility for . . . the basis of most of our lives came through the public schools. That's where we were educated, that's where we got our chance . . . that's what opened up the door . . . however small the doors might have been, they were probably bigger than the ones the generation before us had. And to me it is a civic responsibility not to let an institution that has been very much a part of the development of this country and its people begin to fall apart."

Within the embattled Kansas City, Missouri, school district is Southwest High School, a hulking brick edifice like Central, but surrounded by a peaceful middle-class neighborhood of neat lawns and modestly comfortable homes. In the mid-seventies during the first desegregation effort many neighborhood children were pulled out of the district and placed in private schools. Today 65 percent of the students—mostly black—are bused in from surrounding areas.   Southwest is considered one of the most promising schools in the city—but, along with the rest of

Kansas City's school system, it is precariously balanced between the larger, polar possibilities we have seen at Central High and Shawnee Mission.

On the struggle of Southwest to reclaim the trust of the middle class, could hang the future of the entire Kansas City school system. This nation of different races and unequal classes, has ventured much in its massive endeavor to educate all of its children. But now, in order to win back the support of the middle class, the schools must prove that the extraordinary democratic venture can work; that one common school system can lead our most gifted children, as well as our disadvantaged students, to achieve their full individual potential. One of the gravest dangers to our public school system over the next decade is the possibility that middle-class parents, black and white, will continue to abandon city schools, taking with them the support, the expectations, the energy, and the leadership those schools so vitally need. The ultimate implications of this division for the nation are harrowing: the institutionalization of a permanent under-educated class, and the sabotage of the central ideal of the American democratic experiment: equal opportunity for all. If that hope, that light dies, we face, in the words of one analyst, "a dangerously combustible future."

That is what the fight is about in Kansas City—and if school systems like Kansas City's are to be saved, it will be because ordinary citizens have decided to breathe their schools back to life. The story of the reform movement of this midwest city could be the story of school reform movements all over the country. Here that movement to lift standards, lift falling test scores, began with parents.

When a group of parents in Kansas City first tried to ask hard questions they found they had to fight a bureaucracy. Karen Lewis, one of the mothers in this group, told about the problem of making oneself heard: "When you'd go to the principal it was downtown's fault. They couldn't do anything because it was those downtown administrators. You'd get downtown . . . Oh, it was board policy. We can't change that. We can't do anything about that, it's board policy."

Another mother, Joyce Stark, said, "The first time some of us did try to change things, we weren't very careful about how we suggested the change. We were somewhat abrasive. We didn't want to hear any more arguments and we didn't want to wait for the next meeting and the next meeting and so there was a period of real friction."

A third, Sue Fulson explained: "We would go meet with people on the board and they would shake their heads and shake their heads, and you'd go to the meeting and wait for something to happen and . . . it never happened . . . and then at some point we began to say—well, we've got to get somebody on the board who . . . who really will vote when the issue comes up . . . and that worked its way around the horn and Joyce was the obvious candidate."

Within a few years, Joyce Stark, Karen Lewis and Sue Fulson were all elected members of the Kansas City school board. Stark eventually became president of this new board; Sue Fulson became treasurer. Karen Lewis explained her purpose at a board meeting: "To revive a school system is an awesome task: to break through the bureaucracy; to build curriculums; to hold the brightest, to regain public confidence."

Today, in selected elementary schools in Kansas City—schools where dedicated parent groups working with top-flight principals have established standards and pleasant working conditions for all—there is a sense that the ideal is within reach, that indeed all children can learn. But in this city, as in this nation, the triumphs are still limited; too many schools are still below standard. Too many teenagers still find themselves struggling with basic readers; too often gains made in elementary schools are lost in Junior and Senior High.

John Goodlad explores this problem: "Consequently the attitude accompanying all of this on the part of the schools was to really lean over backwards to try to move these youngsters along."

In many schools, teachers found minority student unprepared. The teachers lowered expectations for these students led to a lowering of standards in academics, in discipline. Ashton Stovall a member of the reform movement, said, "It's the reverse prejudice . . . that we call it. It's the patting them on the head and saying 'Oh, aren't they cute.' Okay, and not expecting them to actually attain."

Tim Lewis was among the white students from the Southwest neighborhood who went to the public schools. He says, "It was very hard to get used to seeing my friends leaving out of junior high to go to private schools, and thinking, 'Man, it would have been fun to play football with those guys up at Southwest.' But if you were to talk to someone from a local private school they would say, 'Is it dangerous over at your school? Are there as many problems as they say? Is there a chemistry class and a physics class?' Those are the kinds of questions they ask."

Timothy Lewis is a youth of almost relentless decency and wheat-fed wholesomeness, an athlete and top graduate of his class who now is going to Yale. In his graduation address, Tim recounted the long passage of his class through two teachers' strikes, the fears and turmoils of desegregation, the steady migration of white middle-class students to other districts. His mother, Karen of whom we spoke earlier, is one of the leaders of the movement to save Kansas City's public schools, and his sister Katherine and younger brother Johnny are still in the public schools there.

Tim expressed his views: "Obviously there's no danger at Southwest, and there is a chemistry class—there are quite a few, and there are physics classes. There's so much misinformation in the community about the school."

But Tim knows that the fate of Southwest, and thereby, probably, the fate of the city's school system, hangs on whether it will be able to attract and keep children from middle-class homes, because they bring so much else into the school with them: the critical resources of interested parents, the interests of the community. As for himself, Tim warmly reflects on a moment in his weight-lifting class when he fully realized how he had been enriched by sharing school with blacks:

94

"I realized that this was something I couldn't have anywhere else. I actually felt more comfortable with them than I would with a bunch of my white peers, because there was a certain looseness, a certain lack of formality. We really felt comfortable together. . . . And it was something I was never going to get again in my life . . . And it really strengthened my belief that public schools can work . . . That's an environment that a lot of my friends couldn't feel comfortable in, even if they wanted to . . . you learn how to, how to merge the gap between black and white, and poor and rich, and find some common denominator to work on . . . It's something I would never have gotten anywhere else."

At the very heart of public disaffection with the public school system lies the most controversial issue in American education: the continuing breakdown of the school system along racial and class lines, and the failure of the communities of the nation—despite years of integration efforts—to halt that process.

Stephanie Spears, like Timothy Lewis, was a senior at Southwest. She is black; a tall and striking girl who, ever since elementary school, has travelled alongside Tim through Kansas City's integrated system. But her own experience has differed from his. Today she is poised, accomplished and radiantly popular. She was one of the hundreds of black students bused to Southwest out of the black zones of Kansas City, and she can still remember how, at the outset of integration, white teachers expected little of her—did not even bother requiring that she work in study hall or turn in homework. Stephanie became President of the Student Council at Southwest High School and remembers some of her teachers: "It was like they didn't think we were as intelligent . . . like if I didn't study it wasn't like they were going to say, 'Stephanie, aren't you going to study?' It was like maybe they expected me not to study."

A major challenge for our schools is not only to lift expectations for all students, but to bring about a nationwide return to the mastery of fundamentals. Now, in hundreds of districts, standardized tests are being revived that will more accurately measure student achievement. Automatic promotions from grade to grade are being eliminated, graduation requirements are being raised. At the heart of the school reform effort is a new concentration on teaching students to read, write, and speak with logic and clarity.

Ernest Boyer says, "I believe that probably the most important single failing in schools in the curriculum has been the failure to say in the earliest years of education . . . 'the mastery of language and the skillful use of English are the most critically important goals we have to achieve.' "

Southwest principal, Barbara Lusk, brought to office by the reform movement, has achieved mini-miracles. Students and teachers perceive her as fair and determined to raise standards among students and teachers alike. She has little tolerance for the undisciplined, recognizes that too many of her youngsters are still entering high school ill-prepared and is deeply aware that Southwest has remedial courses, insufficient advanced classes, and that this school-like so many others—is apt to give short shrift to the average student. While Lusk struggles to convince the community that Southwest could once again become one of the great institutions in the area, her capacity for reform is limited—by resources, by money. Lusk knows that the schools' best hope are the community committees set up by the reform movement. These committees, made up of parents and community leaders, not only help develop school policies but are trying to offset limited budgets with volunteer help. And they are developing urgently needed partnerships with business leaders such as Henry Block, President and Chief Executive Officer of H&R Block Company. Mr. Block has become a diligent school advocate, earnestly talking about the perils facing a city if the public school system is degraded. A graduate of Southwest, Block is now working with the school. He is trying to upgrade the building, which has not been painted in over twenty years and suffers from an inadequate heating system and a wiring system so primitive the school cannot use electric typewriters in class. Block has promised to underwrite the cost of a calculus class next semester. As Block wanders through the halls of Southwest, he inevitably contrasts the school now to its halcyon years when he was a student, when suburban children from Shawnee Mission would falsify their residency addresses to gain admission to Southwest.

To recover the faith of business leaders, of the community, of middle-class parents, public schools such as Southwest must prove they *can* prepare students for any university in the country. In Southwest's battle for community support, every personal success becomes a school triumph.

On April 16, 1984 notification day for Eastern colleges, Tim Lewis was due to hear from Yale, by whom he was accepted. Stephanie Spears was also waiting to hear from Eastern colleges. Stephanie had already been accepted by the University of Missouri, but her hope was for an Ivy League school. Stephanie confided, "This is the first graduation in years in our family . . . my grandmother has seven grandchildren and I'm the first one to graduate." Even though Stephanie was rejected by Barnard, by Amherst and by Dartmouth. She finally accepted an offer to go to the University of Houston.

Despite those rejections, Stephanie *had* reached a goal which was deeply important not only to her but to her family and to Southwest. She is part of a new generation of black students who go on to college.

Ernest Boyer, President of the Carnegie Foundation for the Advancement of Teaching, commented: "The national report was entitled 'A Nation At Risk.' Didn't say a state at risk. Didn't say a local district. I would assume a national problem of that dimension would stir some national response. The federal role is first to help achieve equity and help provide compensatory help in those schools and districts where children are disadvantaged. The federal program to do that has been going on for fifteen or twenty years. The administration has tried to reduce that money at the very time when we all agree early help perhaps can eliminate problems later on."

But Terrell Bell, the former Secretary of Education, said: "We haven't cut that program. We're spending more money on that program than we ever have in our history. Now whether it's kept up with some of the ravages of inflation or not, I'd have to investigate that further." Yet according to many experts, hundreds of thousands of disadvantaged children are being dropped from these programs. Former Secretary Bell's own Department of Education's most recent figures show that, since 1981, the number of disadvantaged students in special classes designed to help them catch up had declined by more than half-a-million children. Even districts like Shawnee Mission, that do not need federal funds, must now campaign harder to ensure continued taxpayer support. Here in the suburbs, and also in the broad middle range of schools which are neither rich nor poor, there's concern that an aging population could lose interest in the schools.

The strength of all suburban schools is in great measure a consequence of the support of the local communities surrounding them. But in cities, bereft of local support, major financial intervention is needed, if schools are to be salvaged.

In the last analysis, the year of school reform has meant little to the students in the inner cities. Where, national and state education budgets have been reduced. Yet, President Reagan says: "We care about education because we care about you. And we care about you, not just because you are our children and grandchildren, but because you are the future of America—the ones who will carry the torch of freedom and idealism into the twenty-first century—the ones that will keep the American Dream alive."—But across America many youngsters believed they were already trapped outside the dream.

The struggle to save our public schools is finally a struggle for the American democratic promise. It's a struggle that will, be won or lost on the level of every individual community—a struggle to win back the commitment of parents, win back the faith of citizens.

While quarrels continue about teaching methods, about school staffing and the value of testing, there is little argument today about the value of parental and community committment. Whether we save our schools and save our children will largely be decided over the next decade by whether ordinary Americans in communities across the nation will be stirred enough to provide the support needed to rescue the public schools. Whether we are willing to move beyond old differences of race and class that not only divide our neighborhoods, but also our schools. That is the great problem now confronting those battling for reform—and the not incidental democratic adventure they have embarked on.

The diminution of parental and community commitment are a very real peril to the survival of our public school system. The compounding alarms about the state of our schools have generated a clamor for reform. But educators alone cannot resurrect public education in this country.

Where those volunteer groups have formed and defined their true goals, they identify and encourage the good teachers, try to sift out the bad; they learn how to cut through endless debates over curriculum, through the semantic entanglements of standard educationese, and through the elaborate baffling inertias of educational bureaucracies.

But, like so many volunteer efforts, the current movements of parents and civic leaders may have too narrow a base to survive the magnitude of the challenge facing them. As a result of the staggeringly expanded democratic mission consigned to schools over the last few decades, the city schools, especially, despite their limited means and support, must struggle to educate the most heterogeneous collection of students ever assembled. The attempt to conduct through high school the marginal student—those students who, as recently as a generation ago, might have passed from elementary school into manual work on the farm or in the factory—is a formidible task complicating the reform movement in our high schools.

11. Curriculum Consensus

Elemental to all initiatives for reform must be community consensus on just what constitutes a basic education. That may seem on the surface a simplistic question. But it implicitly involves fundamental issues. Today there reigns confusion and heated differences over what all children should learn and how it should be taught.

For we are moving into a world of the most fierce competition. A world in which America's strength must begin—as it always has—in the minds of our children, in our public schools.

Dr. Diane Ravitch of Teachers College, tells of such needs: "Moving as we are into the twenty-first century, we want to have a population that is literate in math and science. We want every individual to have the resources, the mental resources to make choices, to change a vocation if his job becomes technologically obsolete. And the fact that a child comes from a poor home is not a rationale for not teaching him. We want people with mental agility, and we want a population that can use language intelligently. We want people with the knowledge of history so that they know who they are and what our country is."

In our public schools are those who will write our laws, will build our cities, will shape the destiny of America. Our future will lie in the skill of their minds, in their sense of humanity and of the democratic ideal.

Beyond the common agreement that all students must learn basically how to read, how to write, how to calculate, there lies considerable controversy over how far that core curriculum can reach. Can poor children from disadvantaged homes be expected to work on the level of college-bound students from enriched environments?

While, on a national scale, there has been genuine improvement over the years in conventional literacy—defined as anyone who has passed a sixth grade education—the real *functional* literacy of Americans in critical areas of cognitive and language skills is poor. This is true of middle-class students as well as the disadvantaged.

However, it is more pronounced among the disadvantaged. Today functional illiteracy among teenage blacks exceeds 40 percent, at a time when society is growing increasingly complex and these skills are more necessary than ever. A debate has raged for many years over the learning deficits placed on an underclass child and, by extension, on his or her school—over not even how much, but indeed *whether at all*, the teacher could overcome the deprived homelife.

Though this debate has yet to be settled. Most recently studies show that the right type of individualized instruction *can* work wonders on underclass children. Because there are not the funds or the teachers available to individualize instruction as needed to help poor and minority children, these pupils remain without needed skills and emotional maturity. For them, learning as usual just will not do. Even if a teacher could help one or two, few ways have been found to cope simultaneously with thirty-five children who are developmentally and socially immature. Often the cycle worsens, and whatever hope there is of raising the academic level of these students succumbs to the inability or unwillingness of the system and the public to go the extra distance necessary to help these children achieve. Thus, education falters in our urban schools because overburdened school cannot solve the problems of today and tomorrow on yesterday's resources.

As to whether these children *could* learn as much as children from stable, middle-class homes, under the present state of affairs we may never know. As to whether they *should*, the less we answer yes, the more do we abandon our hopes for a country in which the poor have any real hope of escaping their condition.

Where dedicated educators are jointed by dedicated school advocates and are provided with a reasonable budget, the difference is remarkable. Schools with widely heterogeneous students *have* been made to work; poor, underprivileged children have demonstrated a dramatic capacity to learn. But what is dismayingly evident is that, while a handful of ardent school advocates can make an almost miraculous difference within a given school, these are isolated pockets of triumph, only glimpses of a possibility, rather than a widespread reality. The struggle for real reform where it finally counts, at the immediate level of individual communities, remains a fragile and uncertain battle.

Thirty years after *Brown vs. Board of Education*, many of America's public school systems remain separate and unequal in many cities. Numerous inner city schools have become ghettoes of disadvantaged students, dispirited teachers. The worst of these schools are custodial day-care centers for adolescents; scholastic slums that perpetuate stereotypes of failure.

These are the schools that were abandoned as the middle class shifted their children to private schools and suburbs. So began a distressing new pattern of resegregation. Behind that flight lay a regretable assumption: that the attempt to educate the under-privileged alongside the best and the brightest would debase the quality of education altogether. And despite successes that prove children of widely-mixed backgrounds can be given an excellent basic education together, that suspicion has endured.

Now the difficulties of class division in the public school systems are amplifying—and in the coming decade will be profoundly altered—by the sheer weight of population shifts occurring in many parts of the country. The proportionately higher birth rates of minorities pose the very real possibility that, by the end of the decade, minority children will be nearing the majority in America's schools. The struggle to be waged during the coming decade—will be to halt the splitting of our school system; to find a way to maintain the quality of our schools and provide equal opportunity for all; and basically, to preserve that belief in public education for all children in communities across the nation which is so vital in achieving these goals. These are the specific challenges we are about to face:

■ A steady dwindling of those young, middle-class parents and taxpayers upon whom the public schools have so heavily depended in the past.

■ The emerging of a preponderately different student population over the next decade, fueled by a birth rate which, for the disadvantaged and minorities, climbs earlier and higher than it does for the middle class. In addition a larger proponent of immigrant children who will pose language and assimilation problems for already beleaquered and understaffed schools.

■ Collectively, minorities in six years will constitute nationally more than 30 percent of the children in our public schools. The projections for major urban areas are even more startling: In our twenty-five largest cities, only one student in ten belonged to a minority in 1950; in 1960 this had grown to one in three; in 1970, to one of every two; by 1980 the numbers had been reversed and seven out of ten students were from our nation's minorities; by 1990, we will have come full circle, with only one student in ten *not* black, Hispanic or Oriental. Already, in many states, the numbers of school-age children from minority backgrounds are climbing: 57 percent in New Mexico, 46 percent in Texas; 43 percent in California; 33 percent in Arizona and Maryland; 32 percent in New York State.

These profound student shifts will present a staggering challenge to the survival of the American public school system—and to our own democratic commitment. They also pose a central and potentially tragic irony: all the strains and dislocations of the massive effort to more widely democratize our schools and fulfill the American promise of equal opportunity for all our peoples, are precisely one reason so many Americans—out of impatience, caution, racial fears—are fleeing many of those schools for the sanctuaries of all-white outer suburbs or alternative private systems. Thus, the grand democratic mission consigned to the public schools over the last few decades—what could be considered their second, great Jeffersonian task—threatens now to produce exactly the reverse effect: not only a more deeply divided school system, but more deeply divided communities.

In the past, for middle-class America, public education seemed a secure enough American institution though inequities were numerous. An unspeakable commentary on this nation would be if, in trying to rectify those old inequities and divisions, we should wind up not only returning to them more implacably, but actually destroying the meaning of the public school system itself through a failure of belief, or will, to make the grand but difficult venture work. And that failure could confirm the division of America itself into two countries—the country of the privileged, and the country of the dispossessed. That, ultimately, is what's at stake over the next decade in meeting our educational challenge.

George H. Hanford, President of the College Board, noted, in September, 1985, that although the SAT scores of Blacks rose in 1985, the number of Black students taking the test declined by about 2000. "When this fall-off in numbers is coupled with other data we have gathered on the educational attainments of Blacks, the decline is disturbing," he said.

Moreover, although the National Assessment of Educational Progress report, issued in September 1985, states that there has been improvement in the reading level of the 250,000 students sampled, seventeen year-old Black and Hispanic students still read only at the level of thirteen year old white students. Gains made by all students leveled off after 1980 and there was almost no progress for students in advantaged urban schools from 1971 to 1984. Thus, budget cutbacks effecting programs such as Headstart may wipe out the gains of earlier years for younger disadvantaged youngsters, while the fact that only 5% of older students can read college-geared textbooks, surely bodes trouble for those seeking higher educations.

In the particular battle to rescue the public school system now underway in Kansas City, Missouri, we find the legacy, in microcosm, of the troubled history of our country's schools over the last several decades: what the nation has attempted, what we have achieved, where we have failed. And the struggle in Kansas City also offers hints of what the future may ultimately require of communities like it across America, and of our governments, if we are to save our schools and save our children from the blighting, wasting divisions of race and class.

104

PART IV

The Perilous Decade:

THE FINAL PERIL

"They're going to be voting, they're going to be determining
our future and in order to do that in our kind of society, they
need to have a level of understanding of history . . . of government, of man's humanity to man, which is part and parcel
of the educative process and I don't think we can leave all that
to chance."

Dr. John Goodlad

This country has embarked on an extraordinary mission—to
educate all our children; to school even those marginal students
who but a generation ago passed from elementary school into
manual work on the farm or in the factory. Diane Ravitch points
out that "the schools are being asked today to do what they've
never been asked to do before, to educate all children in a way
that up until now only out best children were educated." To
provide a basic education for every youngster until the age of
sixteen, in a society as heterogeneous as ours, is an awesome
task. The ultimate question now—will Americans with relative
affluence and political power be willing to support public education for those unable to provide that support for themselves.

But the battle for the public schools today is not just a battle
for bigger budgets. We have committed ourselves to a national
school system without ever defining what that education should
be. In any given school, standards are often more reflective of
a youngster's economic status than his intellectual potential. Be-

yond the common agreement that all must learn how to read, write and calculate, lies considerable controversy. Can students from disadvantaged homes be expected to work on the same level as the college-bound, from homes with academic traditions? Should a school with limited resources favor the gifted—or those most in need of help?

The crisis in public education today, says Dr. Ernest Boyer, is a basic "confusion over goals." For many communities, for many school districts these fundamental questions have never been resolved in part because they directly reflect our attitudes towards class and race.

In the Shawnee Mission District, where there are large numbers of well-prepared middle-class students, the community has high intellectual expectations. Parents and students expect the schools will emphasize traditional academic courses and there is little talk of the need for manual training. The only real debate in affluent communities is over ways to motivate students in the scholastic middle third, those who would spend their high school years floating through class.

But across the state line in Kansas City, Missouri, the problems are far more diffuse and harder to engage. Where schools are obligated not only to prepare the college bound but also are responsible for large numbers of students from disadvantaged backgrounds there remains confusion, racial self-consciousness and heated differences over what these children can learn and how they should be taught. "You have a school full of low income youngsters" says Dr. Theodore Sizer, "and the temptation is to say well we will give them good technical training and they'll learn to use their hands . . . Social class is the least talked about, most serious American problem which we have in the eighties . . ."

It is expected that youngsters in an affluent suburban high school will perform at a sophisticated level—and they are given the scholastic tools they need to do so. They have the books, the teachers, the science laboratories, and for those who fall behind there are tutors and counselors and staff psychologists for support.

Youngsters from disadvantaged homes all too often attend disadvantaged schools. "Low income youngsters in high schools," Sizer reports, "face teachers who carry loads of a hundred and seventy five kids a day . . . but you move out to the suburbs, those loads may be anywhere from eighty to a hundred and ten youngsters. . . . The wealthier youngster gets more personal attention."

Depressed high schools like Central High, in Kansas City, Missouri have great difficulty in attracting talented staff while across the state line in the Shawnee District principals can choose from among the best candidates in the region. As the numbers of minority students and youngsters from families below the poverty line has increased, the divisions within our national school system have sharpened. In 53 of our largest cities, non-whites will be in the majority by 1990, many from disadvantaged homes. Race, class, now threaten to break our public school system apart. In many of our major cities today, the long desegregation struggle has been halted. Despite significant gains in the last twenty years, in one large urban area after another, particularly in the cities of the Northeast and the South, public schools are resegregating. America now confronts an inescapable challenge to its democratic meaning.

Seventeen years ago, following the worst racial convulsions this country has ever seen, a presidential commission declared that America was moving toward two societies, one black, one white—separate and unequal. The report warned of the grim conditions of inner-city schools. Our neglect of those warnings has now imperiled us all, and we are confronted with a hard decision: either we move, through our schools, to build one common American neighborhood or America could move further toward fracturing into two societies—one explosively unequal to the other. That second America is emerging most ominously in our central cities where one out of every four students comes from an impoverished family—where Black and Hispanic students are clustered in highly segregated underfunded schools—where the drop-out rates can exceed 50 percent among

Spanish-speaking youngsters. In these city schools one sees most starkly the schism in American society. As well as the confusion over what constitutes a basic education.

Ernest Boyer, President of the Carnegie Foundation for the Advancement of Teaching, expands upon these issues: "If you have one group of students who become empowered through education—that is, they can use language effectively by which they can understand the issues and can debate them and have enough confidence to know how to participate actively . . . and on the other hand you have students who have simply marked time for four years, who haven't gained any degree of confidence or skill . . . then we've built a two-class system in which people with power control the lives of the unempowered.

"That's not only not good democracy and not good government, it's disastrous social policy. In the end, those who don't have the authority will become increasingly angry that they can't participate and help shape their own destiny. The end would be a crisis and confrontation and, I think, a dramatic erosion in the dream we call America."

The impetus to integrate America's public schools grew in large measure out of a desire to integrate a disparate society of races *and* classes; to develop a common culture; to give all our children an equal educational opportunity. But thirty years after *Brown vs. Board of Education,* all too many of America's largest public school districts have become ghettoes of disadvantaged students and dispirited teachers. There are high schools now that are little more than custodial day-care centers for adolescents—scholastic slums that perpetuate racial stereotypes and class differences. With old racial suspicions still at work among us, the profound racial shifts in our cities will present a staggering challenge to the survival of the American public school system and to our own democratic commitment.

The irony is that in many communities desegregation has worked. Almost 40 percent of all black students *do* study in well-integrated schools. There *is* a growing black middle class. And while national SAT scores went down between the mid 1970s and the mid 1980s, there was a dramatic improvement in the scores of black students—narrowing the scholastic gap between black and white.

Now there is a critical race between that hopeful promise, and the growing numbers of disadvantaged youngsters and disadvantaged school systems. The battle to rescue the urban school system in Kansas City, Missouri, mirrors the struggle of other city districts-districts where the middle class has fled, leaving the poor behind-where there simply is not the population mix needed to integrate the schools.

Nationally, where the federal government and the courts have been most assertive—systematic segregation in the schools has been greatly reduced. But in many other regions where the courts have been far more ambivalent, *de facto* segregation not only remains entrenched, but is spreading. Almost half of all the black students in the Northeast study in schools that are overwhelmingly (90-100 percent) minority.

In 1977, the Kansas City student population was over 65 percent non white, with a high percent of families below the poverty line. A group of parents, led by Joyce Stark with the help of the NAACP Legal defense Fund, tried to break down the wall between city and suburbs—black and white, rich and poor—by suing to incorporate the more affluent white districts around them into one common system. The suburbs fought back these efforts to erase the district lines that insulated their schools, their children.

The suit trailed on for over seven years, exhausting the reformers, reducing the local attorney to the edge of bankruptcy. By early 1985, without sufficient state or federal funding, unable to raise enough community support, Kansas City—like so many other cities—seemed destined to continue with separate and unequal schools.

Last year, Ruby Jackson, a long time fighter for school reform, was deeply discouraged. "I believe," she said "we're in trouble. We said public education and we really mean public, we mean all races, we mean disabled, we mean everybody. That takes

111

money. Do we want to be taxed to really have a public education that's good for all people? You know, these are things that really have to be answered by people like you and me in order to make the push so that politically we can get the type of education we want. Therefore, it's just a big question in my mind. Are we able? Will we do it?''

Those long fighting for integration show both defiance and fatigue. For the first time since the fifties they have found themselves pitted not only against the resources of the affluent communities they are trying to join, but also up against the might of the federal government and the Justice Department.

The resistance to integration grows primarily out of the long-standing assumption that any attempt to educate the underprivileged alongside the best and the brightest will inevitably debase the quality of education. Long-standing prejudices persist in spite of solid evidence that children of widely-mixed backgrounds *can* be given an excellent basic education in one common school. Across America there are glimpses of how that awesome democratic mission has been made to work.

To wander through the classes of Borderstar Elementary School in Kansas City, Missouri, is to remember what the old dream of integrated education was all about. Poor and rich children learn side-by-side. In the intensity of learning, racial and economic lines blur. The school is a lively mix of affluent neighborhood children as well as inner-city children bused in from the black corridor. The younger classes are *not* tracked by ability, but, instead, well-trained teachers use informal clustering within each class to allow each child to move at his own rate. A dedicated principal has imbued in her students and staff a sense of purpose and pride. Six years ago, when Jesse Kirksey first took over Borderstar, she says, ''we had teachers who really believed that minority children couldn't learn, we had parents who believed their children couldn't learn, we even had children feeling they couldn't learn.''

There has been a revolution in expectations at Borderstar. Every child is expected to learn how to read—and every child learns how to read—most above the national norm. The limited school budget is augmented by dedicated parent volunteers. A general science class is conducted by a parent; local business men provide time, money and expertise. There is a sense of expectation that fuels the spirit—*and* the learning curves. At Borderstar, poverty is not an excuse.

Clearly it is easier to reform an elementary school than a high school. Yet a lanky adolescent struggling over a third grade reader understands all too well that he's been prepared for little more than filling out unemployment forms. But if the children of Borderstar are to build on the basic skills they now celebrate, they must be able to move on to upper schools capable of consolidating their education; they must have access to teaching that can prepare them for an ever-more complex world.

"Moving as we are into the 21st century," says Dr. Diane Ravitch, Professor of History at Teachers College, "we want to have a population that is literate in math and science. We want every individual to have the mental resources to make choices, to change a vocation if his job becomes technologically obsolete. We want people with mental agility, and we want a population that can use language intelligently. We want people with the knowledge of history so that they know who they are and what our country is."

In our public schools today are those who will write our laws, who will build our cities, who will shape the destiny of America. Our future will lie in the skill of their minds in their sense of humanity and of the democratic ideal. The public schools were to be the common school for democracy. The open doorway to the American promise. They were to forge a larger American community out of our wide diversity of races and classes. But as middle America mobilizes to protect its schools, the fundamental question remains, who will pay for the schooling for the other Americans?

Every June, all over this country from the smallest rural hamlet to the grimmest corner of the inner city, students and families share an extraordinary American ceremony—the high school graduation. Behind the rhetoric—the pomp and circumstance—the tassles on the mortar boards that never hang quite right, lie the dreams. But seventeen-year-olds are also rooted in reality, understand well the political and philosophic conflicts that have surrounded them since kindergarten.

At Central High, in Kansas City, the graduation address—"Against All Odds," dealt with life in the ghetto, with racism, and poverty, crime and drugs and infant mortality rates. There was singing and expressions of hope and Barry Bailey paid tribute to his father, and tried to look beyond the dismal corridors of his school. "You just have to go on with your ideals and your dreams and your aspirations and you have to do the best you feel you can do. . . . ." There was also a clear sense that Bailey and those he'd struggled with for twelve years of schooling were never given the academic tools they need. Demographics and the realities of public education prematurely limited their aspirations.

At Southwest High School in Kansas City, Timothy Lewis knew that while his own education was solid many of his classmates were far less fortunate. Together the class had faced two teachers' strikes, the fears and turmoils of desegregation, the steady migration of white middle-class students to other districts. They had lived through a period of falling standards and the attempted reformation that followed. For Tim, at the top of his class there was a real sense of triumph, "We have perservered and those of us who graduate tonight are proof that barriers can be overcome." Other students were less fortunate. Some caught in changing standards found themselves without the credits to graduate.

In the summer of 1985, a federal district judge in Kansas City moved to settle the fate of that city's schools. He ordered an $87 million plan to upgrade the district. Over the next three years, the State of Missouri will be required to spend four times the money that had been budgeted for Kansas City schools. The judge called for voluntary integration with the Missouri suburban schools but the suburbs are resisting and *that* problem has yet to be resolved. For the school reformers in Kansas City there is a sense of triumph. That small, heroic band of parents who for so many years gave up so much of their personal time and energy. For years they have been studying *how* to upgrade their schools. Now, with the funds at hand, their priorities and goals are clear. Class sizes can be reduced, additional teachers and counselors can be hired. Academic courses can be increased, and so can the remedial staff. Finally, there is a sense that the schools in the inner corridor can be turned back into centers of learning; that the next generation of youngsters and their teachers might well move through this system with greater assurance, a greater sense of purpose, a greater sense of belonging to a wider community.

But in many other urban areas, millions of poor and minority children remain in forgotten ghettoes, isolated in separate schools, the unseen children of another America. Their neglect now threatens this nation's economic strength, and the very democratic soul of our Republic.

That's the danger—the final peril.

PART V

The Perilous Decade:

CANDLES IN THE DARKNESS

10

STUDENTS——

9

Electronically charged by drugs, alcohol, TV and sex . . .

8

Haphazard, unregulated, sometimes dangerously uncared for, socially and emotionally deprived . . .

7

FAMILIES——

6

Disoriented, dissolving, deserting public schools . . .

5

TEACHERS——

4

Dispirited, overburdened and poorly paid . . .

3

Inadequately trained or burned out . . .

2

SCHOOLS——

1

Without needed public or government support . . .

"ZERO"

This is our zero hour. Either we are poised on the brink of explosion and eventual darkness, or we must launch our vessel—public education—into unexplored new horizons of learning and achievement.

Our nation's future has already begun to take shape in the minds of our children. Thus, it is largely in the hands of our schools. And across America millions of parents, educators and politicians have been alerted to hazardous threats posed by the crisis in our public school system—to violence in schools making headlines; to video fever amidst the young; to depression among students accounting for epidemic teen suicides; to wavering test scores, to massive drop-outs of high school students, not only in inner cities, but in the rural areas of Louisiana, Mississippi, Tennessee, Florida, Georgia and South Carolina. They've been alerted to alarming statistics—to one-fifth or more adult Americans being functionally illiterate; to high school graduates suing because they are unable to fill out job applications; to growing numbers of abandoned, neglected and abused children of every age, among every economic class; to being, indeed, a nation at risk.

The multi-faceted crisis in our schools casts a long shadow. Today's poorly-educated children will be tomorrow's ill-prepared citizens—unable to meet technological, global or economic challenges. Mediocrity in our schools means that, in an era where each day brings immense national and international perils, we shall have a nation where people can not read or write, think or analyze, make intelligent decisions, adjust to scientific and societal changes, or absorb critical new ideas.

Yet, despite the growing darkness which threatens us, some have lit candles. They create faint glimmers of light by which we might, if only they could be clearly seen, chart our course. These creative and innovative illuminators have sprung up in defiance of budget cuts, waning community support, the decaying teaching profession and problematic students. Concern about this country's lost educational superiority has already produced the nebula of attitudes, policies and actions that are most likely to cause reform in the schools. These new programs and ideas have emerged from many segments of society:

■ From individual people:

People like H. Ross Perot have emerged to begin the reconstruction of whole school systems and reorder priorities. Mr. Perot, best known for his successful rescue of his employees held hostage in Iran, heads a commission to improve the public education system in Texas. Mr. Perot's suggestions were enacted by a special session of the state legislature in 1984. Most attention has focused on a rule that students must have passing grades in order for them to participate in extracurricular affairs. But an equally important part of Mr. Perot's reform recommendations is using the power of the state to equalize per-student spending on education in rich and poor student districts.

■ From politics:

In New Jersey—where allocation of state money to higher educational institutions was determined primarily by enrollment considerations—T. Edward Hollander, the state's higher education chancellor, has devised a more imaginative system of budgeting. A sizeable sum is now reserved for special project areas determined, not by individual institutions, but by the state. Nearly half of it will go to new initiatives in technology and computer sciences. Another segment is targeted for urban problems, and a third is aimed at strengthening humanities and foreign language instruction.

Thus, upgrading a school system with only fair funding is possible through strategic planning. This same state is beginning a major urban-school initiative to help marginal students meet state graduation requirements.

In California, a new merit-school proposal rewards schools for better attendance, decreased drop-out rates, more homework and more difficult classes.

In New York, full-day kindergartens which were launched

121

citywide in 1983 now serve 60,000 pupils—14,000 more than had attended previous half-day programs—thus providing day-care for a number of younger children found to be emotionally and physically at risk.

Finally, our nation's governors' State of the State messages delivered to their legislatures in 1984 consistently echoed a dominant theme calling for excellence in education. Textbooks, graduation requirements, career ladders, and performance-based pay for teachers were all to be studied. Such movements by the states' leaders combined with those of senators and representatives in Washington could provide the key to a successful educational reform movement nationwide. As a result, forty-eight states are now considering new high school graduation requirements while thirty-five have already approved some changes. Twenty-one states have reported initiatives to improve textbooks and instructional materials, while eight have approved lengthening the school day, seven have approved lengthening the school year, and eighteen have mandates affecting the amount of time for instruction.

■ From corporate initiatives:

Bank of America's grants for creative proposals; Chase Manhattan Bank's support of leadership training for principals; the Boston Compact between private industry and urban public schools to increase high school graduation rates and to provide jobs or post-secondary education for all high school graduates; Atlantic Richfield's involvement in the Carnegie Foundation's high school study, and Arco's millions of dollars to help implement the study's recommendations by generous disbursements to schools—all demonstrate a willingness to move ahead. Eighteen hundred and fifty corporate day-care centers now exist, compared to one hundred in 1978, and compensate—if only in small part—for cutbacks in direct federal subsidies for child care which were slashed by 14 percent in 1981, and have been only to date partially restored.

Millions of dollars have been given in support of local education foundations and to such innovative efforts as national ad-

vertising campaigns and partnership programs which involve employees, company officers and even stockholders in school reform. Corporate publishers have committed $3 million to improve
literacy. Major firms have made significant donations of computer
equipment, including one gift of $12 million in computers to
twenty-six cities. To improve mathematics teaching, one major
oil corporation has awarded $6.7 million for state-of-the-art films
and materials.

There are very impressive efforts in which corporate America
has embraced the educational reform movement. The District of
Columbia public schools have secured the support of eleven major
corporations to establish a management institute to help principals
and administrators sharpen their school management skills. The
California Business Roundtable funded a costly independent
study of how to improve California public schools and strongly
voiced its support for legislative educational reform.

More than 400,000 business representatives serve on nearly
40,000 vocational education advisory councils, while nearly
8,000 Future Farmers of America clubs across the country profit
from thousands of working farmers lending their expertise. And
in an innovative program affectionately referred to as "Adopt A
School," thousands of businesses, civic groups and trade unions
across the country have offered students and faculties guest speakers, field trips, counseling, tutoring and summer internships. In
Los Angeles and Oakland alone, over 200 employers have
adopted schools.

■ From civic groups:
Groups such as the Junior League have projects including a
demonstration child-care subsidy program, referral operations and
after-school telephone support services for latchkey children.

■ From labor:
Labor unions have begun to sponsor kids for day-care scholarships. In some cases they provide volunteers, in others they
furnish space for day care centers.

123

■ From parents:

Such as those parents in Reston, Virginia, who formed a non-profit day-care center that now serves three hundred children and is still owned by the parents. In Des Moines, Iowa, Tiny Tot Child Care, Inc. has become a model of inner-city child care because its founder, Evelyn Davis, sought—and was given—parental support.

■ From school districts:

School districts throughout the country have set up more than a thousand magnet schools to focus on certain subjects or pedagogical approaches, attracting students who might otherwise have been added to our growing list of high school drop-outs or delinquents. At the high school level, for example, magnet schools have been created that emphasize science, mathematics and international affairs. Cincinnati operates magnet schools at the elementary level which concentrate on second-language fluency. In West Roxbury, Massachusetts, the Dr. Wm. H. Ohrenberger School attracts pupils of varied racial backgrounds. At this school, parent-helper programs were established whereby parents tutor absentee children, assist the teacher with clerical tasks, and teach in the pre-kindergarten.

■ From teachers:

Our teachers most of all, provide the system with thousands of dedicated and skilled professionals who are able—despite immense problems within and without their profession—to be innovative and produce the specialized programs which are needed within the public school system so that crucial reform can take place. Among their heartening responses are many commendable efforts. For instance, In November of 1983, the Forum of Educational Organization Leaders—among its ranks are included PTA's, schools, teachers' unions, top state school officials, school boards, and school principals—issued a joint response endorsing specific actions to be initiated in relation to curriculum,

use of school time, testing and evaluation, and teaching. The leaders of both the NEA and the AFT have actively participated in debates regarding the issue of performance-based pay. Outstanding private schools have recently been recognized as a result of a new effort by the Council for American Private Education. Leaders of our nation's schools have created a broad-based Commission on Teacher Education to study fundamental reforms in teacher-preparation programs. And some of these leaders in cities such as Boston and Atlanta are embracing the corporate community as well as colleges and universities in an effort to improve education. And, a review of leading professional journals—several published by educational associations—between Spring of 1983 and the Fall of 1984, show over a hundred articles appearing in response to various reports on teaching, curriculum content, expectations, time, leadership, and fiscal support.

In June and July, 1985, both major unions altered their positions. The National Education Association (NEA) voted to support dismissal proceedings against incompetent teachers and competency exams for all new teachers. In addition, the NEA opened the door to possible approval of merit pay increases. Albert Shanker, president of the American Federation of Teachers, proposed that merit pay be awarded to experienced teachers based on nationwide tests and standards.

In the pages that follow, some of the innovative programs now being used to effect crucial reforms in the areas pin-pointed by the unions and in this book are presented. These areas of concern are first, the students: latchkey children, special concerns of the disadvantaged students, older pupils and addictive diversions. The second area is that of the teachers: the ways in which they are overburdened and underpaid, the ways in which they are unqualified, the facts about their exodus. The third area of concern is lastly, the problem of waning public support.

Although only a limited number of innovative ideas and programs from representative schools are depicted, they strike directly at the problems encountered everywhere and illustrate the way school systems may reverse their downhill slide—not by demanding hugh amounts of public funds amidst the realities of federal and state budget cuts; not by calling for stable family life amidst the realities of ever-increasing numbers of single-parent homes and the need for these parents to be self-supporting; not by throwing the blame for school problems on the shoulders of the overburdened and increasingly powerless figure at the front of the classroom amidst the realities of massive teacher and administrative shortages; not by creating nostalgia for lost days of cheering public faith amidst reports that the middle class is deserting schools. Not by any of these unrealistic, counter productive offsprings of wishful thinking but by addressing the real issues, formulating reform priorities, becoming involved in community and instituting pragmatic programs for schools that are under-funded, as well as schools that are amply funded.

It can be done.

Indeed, the astonishing triumph of the programs that we cite amidst the difficult social and economic conditions in which they exist prove anew the old Chinese proverb:

It is better to light a candle
Than to curse the darkness.

EPILOGUE:

To Save Our Schools, To Save Our Children

Whether we save our schools and save our children will largely be decided over the next decade by you and me—in our own communities over the nation. Either the recent educational reforms will expire or they will ignite lanterns to lead those who care enough about rescuing our schools to solve the complex problems dimming the American ideal of public education. The components of these issues are a sinister presence: the growing population of neglected, alienated, disconnected students; the emergence of a new, different student majority, increasingly from fragmented homes, increasingly minority, poorer, more culturally impoverished; a generation of fewer and less-fit teachers to cope with these more difficult children; a mounting majority of childless or aging Americans with no direct connection to the public schools at all, and therefore, little interest in their fate; a widening disaffection with public schools among taxpayers in general, portending a progressive abandonment of the schools by those who principally supported them in the past. These are the alarming threats which cast long shadows across the very doors through which American children pass into the schools for another year. Our whole tradition of public education itself is poised at the gateway of a decade of danger.

The major menace which must be overcome is the splitting of our school system into two—one small, superior and mostly white; the other larger, poorer, filled mostly with minority children who appear condemned to a wasteland of mediocrity. Some see these newcomers as the ominous otherness against which tradition struggles. Yet it is the very diversity of this underclass which has in the past—and can in the future—illuminate the American ideal; that through education the nation will provide equal opportunity for all. And it reveals another deeply-felt ideal that through education, the nation will realize its faith in progress, ambition, every individual's possibilities for a better life.

The nearly forty-million pupils in our schools—disadvantaged and advantaged—are, in a final sense, all our children. On them, on their awakening, the kinetic energy of their youth, the enlightening of their minds, the potentially enriching gifts of their talents hangs nothing less than America's hope for the lasting political health of our democratic republic, our economic and scientific strength, our position and relevance in the world. As America moves into the complicating uncertainties of the 21st Century, what happens to the children in the public schools of this country will largely determine what happens to this country. It's that simple. It's that complex.

Today we are faced with immense technological and global challenges, the sudden obsolescence of skills, the awesome discoveries of genetic engineering and nuclear science. In the midst of such sweeping breakthroughs, our citizens must be able to read and write, think and analyze, make intelligent decisions and deal effectively with others. Most important is a citizenry who will be able to adjust to change and evaluate new ideas. Moreover, whatever the challenges of today are, tomorrow's will be greater in magnitude, wider in scope. Today's visions will become tomorrow's realities as our children voyage into the future.

The decade to come will be a hazardous passageway along which are found a powerful combination of perils—fundamental, underlying, some already in place but worsening, some less obvious than the ones with which we are now publicly concerned.

128

These demons—both known and unknown—we must confront and surmount if we are to remain a vital, evolving nation.

Whether we can save our school and save our future will, in truth, be determined, not by words but by action; not by dreams but by fundamental reform. Our schools need—in addition to governmental support—community, corporate and private co-operation. Across America, those who care about our destiny must assemble in the active and cohesive volunteer coalitions it will take to resurrect quality public education. For, like so many volunteer efforts, the current government of parents, business and civic leaders may have, against the magnitude of challenges facing them, too narrow a base to survive.

Instead, the light of reforms now begun must kindle broader challenges. The small successes, the modest rise in test scores, the preschool programs which aid the disadvantaged, the cooperative ventures of business and education must continue. Our beginning is a precarious one. For despite these tentative signs of recovery, mounting demands, dwindling monies, disconnected students, and embattled teachers are still recurrent threats which, if not halted will converge crisis during the next decade. And if our current piecemeal reforms do not become part of systematic change toward long-term goals, then they are meaningless. For those small gains will most certainly soon be swept away by a crushing wave of new problems.

In order to maintain and broaden the energies now mobilizing for school change, there must be give and take. If the schools need society's support, the schools must reach out to society in order to construct a permanent interchange between the community and its schools. New collaborative bonds must be formed between an aging, childless population and the young. They must both embark on projects to aid the economic and social well-being of their nation. The value of schools must extend beyond classrooms and bolster the economic health of their communities. In strengthening their surrounding neighborhoods, the schools will strengthen themselves.

Our schools have the vast democratic mission to carry all our children—black, brown, yellow and white, rich and poor, handicapped and gifted—toward the fulfillment of their true potentials. And in this way we can reforge the inseperable link between public education and a free, open, upwardly-mobile society. In order to fulfill this goal, our schools must turn crisis into opportunity, handicaps into challenges, and both failure and success into reasons for continued striving and endeavor.

This staggering academic and social mission is of a scale never before undertaken by any country on earth. Yet it is imperative for America's future to keep open the avenues of success regardless of a child's origin. To do this we must sustain quality education, and at the same time bring millions of disadvantaged children into our schools. We must fill the social void left by the weakening family. We must recapture the attention of disspirited students and a disheartened public, while rebuilding faltering faith in public education. Ahead of us is an arduous and long journey. If we succeed, we will fortify the democratic ideals to which our country's government, industry and popular will have for so long been committed. We will restore the American dream.

But the problems of American public education are enormous, and they pose for all of us as grave and as important a challenge as the nation has ever faced. There are no quick-fixes, no all-purpose bandages. Instead, there must be a decade of dedication as massive as our effort to put a man on the moon. The costs will be immense, but if our schools fail, we all fail.

APPENDIXES

Innovative Ideas
and Programs

APPENDIX A:

Assisting Latchkey Children

As we have seen, one of the most ominous clouds forewarning future turbulence is the occurrence of latchkey children. It is a storm which is gathering momentum. The old-fashioned definition of family has been replaced by economic and social realities that make such intact families largely a nostalgic dream. Two major facts have disassembled this dream: massive divorce statistics affecting family units, and the surge of working mothers—due in no small part to the fact that by 1980, females headed 19 percent of all households with school-age children. We cannot wait for a return to family stability as confirmation of our illusions of how families ought to be constituted. While we wait, seven million children are being left alone or relegated to chaotic daycare, according to the Children's Defense League. There are too many young minds at stake.

And some have begun to meet the challenge to save them:

■ Community support:

Realizing the critical importance of support networks for latchkey children, such organizations as Parents Anonymous of Connecticut have presented sessions on child care to employees of several large companies in Phoenix, Arizona. The Junior League sponsors projects throughout the country, including an after-school telephone support system for children left alone. Camp Fire has created films to teach self-reliance, as have the Boy

133

Scouts. The largest provider of early childhood educations have been the eighteen thousand church-based centers established by religious groups, operating in church space with assistance from the congregation or outside personnel.

■ Schools:

Once again, the schools themselves have sought answers. Save The Children in Atlanta operates a child-care information and referral service. The School-Age Child Care project at Wellesley College in Massachusetts, directed by Michelle Seligson, provides information, research and technical assistance on the design and implementation of day-care centers. And Project Phone-A-Friend, established by a local branch of the American Association of University Women at State College, Pennsylvania, utilizes adult volunteers to dispense supportive advice to more than forty-five hundred elementary children who live in the area of Pennsylvania State University.

Among the programs focusing on the problem of children with working parents three communities in New Jersey have organized very effective extended day programs. They are: the West Windsor-Plainsboro program, the Union Township Program and the Bridgewater Raritan program.

In West Windsor-Plainsboro, the Extended Day Program is sponsored through the Community Education Program under the leadership of Selma Gore. The three district schools open to students from kindergarten to grade six from seven in the morning until six. According to Ms. Gore, the program is possible because of the strong support of the district supervisor and the principals of the schools involved. It is now in its second year of operation.

Union Township has developed an after school program in cooperation with the Five Points YMCA. Approximately one hundred children from seven elementary schools participate in the program. The cost is seventy-five dollars per month and funds from a community development grant are being used to subsidize part of the tuition for children from low-income families. The Y also provides early morning care, comprehensive child care programs for pre-schoolers and several other after school programs.

One of the early communities to recognize and provide after-school care is Bridgewater-Raritan. During the last ten years this area has provided after school care for many children in the district who require it. Designed to be non-profit, the Cim After-School Program operates during the regular school year and is governed by a parent policy-making board, all costs are covered by the tuition receipts. All of the district's elementary schools now have after-school programs.

■ Business:

A growing number of companies have recognized the need to begin emergency action now—both for their own benefit and that of their employees with children. According to Dana Friedman of the Conference Board, a non-profit business-research firm, approximately 1,850 American companies provide support or actual child-care facilities for their employees. Ms. Friedman says in the article "Day Care in America," in the June 1985 issue of *Reader's Digest*, "Corporate-sponsored day care is the fastest growing employee benefit of the Eighties." Among these companies are IBM, which has funded more than two hundred community-based organizations to help employees gain information and guidance about child care. At Zale's, there is an in-house child-care center which has drawn about 40 percent of Zale's workforce to the company.

In Houston, the public school system and the Houston Committee for Private Sector Maintenance, a business group, have combined their expertise to sponsor programs on coping skills for latchkey children.

Answers must come from major sources, and some already have:

■ Government:

In October of 1984, President Reagan signed into law a $24 million program of federal aid for school-based child care. The new child-care block grant to the states was included in S. 2565, which extended the federal Headstart program for two years. Under this plan, non-profit groups can get help to set up before- and after-school child-care programs for children of working parents; but the need for more such centers is apparent.

Studies in urban areas—such as the Long study of children in Washington, D.C., and their 1983 study for the Department of Family Resources in Montgomery County, Maryland, and similar research—have set the proportion of children under age fourteen who are taking care of themselves or being cared for by siblings at 15-30 percent. This is despite the fact that more states are responding to child-care needs than ever before.

In California, the state has established network of sixty-one agencies to help educate parents about child care, and to provide information for caretakers.

New York has made available five hundred day-care openings for the children of teen-aged mothers who can then go back and finish their schooling. New York has also begun the all-day kindergarten program for sixty thousand pupils.

Massachusetts has begun a major effort to help underpaid day-care workers and to attract qualified people to this field. Governor Dukakis wants the state legislature to spend $7.5 million to upgrade the pay scale in state-controlled day-care centers. If this proposal passes, a 30 percent pay raise for workers is contemplated.

New Jersey has introduced two bills which deal with children's safety and welfare. The first has been sponsored by Assemblywoman Jacqueline Walker whose proposal authorizes boards of education to run school-age care programs. It provides for state aid to supplement parent fees, and establishes a regulatory frame. Children from ages five to sixteen would be enrolled in a before- and after-school program during the school year and for extended hours during holidays and vacation days. The school itself or another site approved by the commissioner of education would house the program. Assemblywoman Walker has asked for an appropriation of $10 million. Any district establishing such a center would also have to establish a Child care Council made up of parents, teachers, citizens and community child care professionals. The second bill has been introduced by Senator Gormley. It establishes a grant program for child care services to be administered through the Department of Human Services. Programs would be held in public or nonpublic buildings before and after school for children ages five to twelve. Parents would pay in accordance with a sliding scale of fees and $500,000 would be appropriated from the state. Both bills have now reached the Revenue, Finance and Appropriation Committee for appraisal.

We know now that Project Headstart pays off, not only for the children who enter the program, but also for the taxpayers who have supported it. In Ypsilanti, Michigan, the High Scope Educational Research Foundation completed a twenty-two-year study of 123 children from low-income families who seemed likely to fail at school. Two-thirds of the group which had attended the preschool Headstart program graduated from high school. Thirty-eight percent of them enrolled in higher education institutions, compared to 21 percent of those in the control group. Fifty-one percent of those with no preschool training had been arrested, as opposed to 31 percent of the preschoolers. Eighteen percent of the Headstart group were on welfare, as compared to 32 percent of the others.

In addition, studies of the needs of latchkey children, reports to state governments, and the establishment of incentive grants for child-care programs have been implemented by several states, including California.

■ Redesigning school programs and curricula:

The Veterans Park Elementary School in Ludlow, Massachusetts, offers an Early Childhood Program to children with special needs. The children are between the ages of three and five and they attend the school using a very flexible time schedule—some attending every day Monday through Friday, others spending only a few hours each week in the program. The curriculum consists of language arts and socialization skills. The purpose of the program is to get these children ready for a successful kindergarten experience.

One important component of the program is home visits made by teachers. Such visits provide critical information about homework environments, personal concerns, and emergency procedures for contacting parents. In some instances, teachers bring the school to children who can't yet adapt to classroom situations. The program's teacher is supported by a speech teacher and physical education teacher, both of whom prepare special programs for these needy children.

At the McCarthy-Towne School in Acton, Massachusetts, we find one of the largest groups of parent volunteers in the country, numbering approximately two hundred. The group is so large that it requires a special co-ordinator to monitor activities—the co-ordinator being another volunteer parent. The volunteers are grouped and assigned to positions that include library aide, office aide, lunchroom aide, clerical aide for the teachers, and assistants for after-school programs.

Another innovative program can be found at Frederick J. Delaney School in Wrentham, Massachusetts, where the aid of local senior citizens is solicited. These are usually persons living on pensions who have both the time and the desire to help teach young children during and after school. At present, the senior citizens work only with kindergarten children, to whom they read in the classrooms. Plans are being made, however, to include older children and their participation in the educational program is about to be expanded to include tutoring.

Similarly, ''The Grandmother Hour'' provides special experiences at the Dyer Elementary School in Whitman, Massachusetts, where a staff of seven grandmothers enjoy teacher-planned visits to the school. Here, they take part in story-telling time. The pupils, their parents and the grandmothers are delighted with the program because it fosters respect for older citizens, opens communications between generations, and provides alternative adult support for children without daily in-depth contact with their working parents.

138

An educational program designed specifically for parents can be found at the Fall Brook School in Leominister Massachusetts. The thrust of this program is to create an effective parent-child relationship, and to heighten parental response to their children's need for survival skills for functioning in parentless situations. This thrust makes the program different from the ones offered in most other schools, where the effort is usually designed to create or foster better home and school relationships. The parents in the Riley group include many single parents. In this program they can develop the awareness they need to become effective parents, they can share their experiences, and learn effective ways to relate to their children. Their children's behavior is clarified, resulting invariably in better parent-child communications. This program runs for just ten weeks and is open to every interested parent in the town.

In Southwick, Massachusetts, at the Southwick Consolidated School, the "Nutrition Unit" was instituted in an attempt to help children understand basic nutrition and encourage them to apply their knowledge of nutrition to their daily lives. It is of special importance for those children who must be responsible for a good deal of their own care. Nutrition education is geared and correlated to all units of study used in the school, from kindergarten through grade six.

The program is unique in its use of portable cooking equipment—a portable oven, hot plate, electric frying pan, blender, electric mixer, ice cream freezer, bowls, measuring spoons, cups—which is collected on a utility cart and wheeled directly into the classrooms where the children can work with the equipment. The children's cooking experiences are brought into play in their English, mathematics, social studies, health and spelling courses.

Similarly, the health program at the Ralph Wheelock School in Medfield, Massachusetts, has a program that teaches students how to take care of their own health and hygiene needs. The school employs a doctor, dentist, dietician, and a nurse, along with film strips and puppet shows to help conduct the program.

Again, this is of special significance for children who must cater to their own needs in the absence of parental figures. At the beginning of each school year, the health care program begins with a pet care contest. The children are always very enthusiastic about getting involved in the contest and the winners receive prizes. Immediately following the contest, the emphasis of the program shifts over to personal care which is taught in the classrooms as part of the total school curriculum.

This same school offers a training program for volunteer tutors called HELP. The program, which is over fourteen years old, consists of twenty-four hours of instruction in teaching such school disciplines as reading, math, and language arts, as well as in counseling those children who need support services. The parent volunteers are trained to tutor individuals or small groups of children and then devote sixty to ninety minutes per week to the tutoring. A monthly open forum, moderated by the school principal (who has been trained in this field), allows exchanges of ideas among parents.

These programs, although only a beginning, focus on a fact educators must now face. This is a world of disintegrating family unity and of economic pressures which force mothers, as well as fathers, to be working parents. In such a world we cannot realistically ask how we can get rid of latchkey children; we must, rather, ask how we can save these children and make them functioning, happy, productive adults.

APPENDIX B:

Aiding Disadvantaged Pupils

Unlike children of the middle class, the children of poverty—especially in our cities—are often doomed to remain prisoners of a long and brutalizing legacy of racism and economic deprivation. Caught in this social undertow, the learning liabilities they bring to school are enormous. From homes in which books are a rarity and any vocabulary of ideas is totally lacking, they have had little chance of the early breadth of experience and development common to their more fortunate peers. Many will sink still further behind unless we break their cycle of poverty through education. And it can be done.

Even now, as our country enters its decade of darkening peril in American education, the flares of success have been ignited. Perhaps the most illuminating news is the glowing 1983 report of the High Scope Educational Research Foundation in Ypsilanti, Michigan. The findings of this twenty-two-year study have proved that giving quality preschool education to disadvantaged children boosts their academic performance, reduces crime and saves taxpayers thousands of dollars. ''. . . quality early-childhood education programs can help poor children overcome later problems,'' declared Dorcas Hardy, assistant secretary of the Department of Health and Human Services, which administers Headstart. And there are other programs with similar success stories, among them:

The S.A.D.I.E. program adopted by Palm Beach County Schools. This plan is based on the ideas of educational philosopher Arnold Geselle and seeks to individualize curriculum and activities based on the needs of disadvantaged children who lag behind in conceptual skills and preparedness. In one of the schools adopting the S.A.D.I.E. approach—West Riviera Elementary School—kindergarteners who are largely from minority backgrounds are reading and writing.

Across the country still other innovative programs have been started by those who will not accept the closed horizons of the youngest of our already ghetto-encapsulated children.

One such program is the team-teaching format of alternative programming for troubled children at The Lee McCabe Elementary School. In addition to traditional programs, this school offers an alternative program to assist those pupils who need help in working out academic, social and emotional problems. The alternative teacher receives specialized training in areas such as group interaction, decision-making and independent thinking insofar as they can be used for dealing with these children's special problems.

While grades one through four are combined in self-contained classrooms, grades five and six—in an effort to assist these pupils in adjusting to the highly-structured junior high school—are grouped separately, with one teacher specializing in reading and sciences, the other specializing in math and social studies. The success of such a team approach has been proved by the effective work of the past several years.

In an attempt to work with the problems of disadvantaged preschoolers, Erving Elementary School in Millers Falls,Massachusetts,has introduced a program for four-year-olds who will be entering the school's regular kindergarten classes. The only requirement for eligibility for the program is only that the child be four years old by December 31 of that year. No funding from federal or state resources is involved in this project, all monies are provided by the local community.

The approach of early primary-grade grouping offers a unique coupling of kindergarten and first grade at the Pine Hill Elementary School in Shelborn, Massachusetts. In looking at similar programs in neighboring communities, several factors appealed to the Pine Hill faculty: The kindergarteners, placed with the only slightly older children in first grade, helped to ease the transition from home to school. The children spend two years with the same teacher, thereby eliminating a large element of the great adjustment period at the beginning of the first grade year. The first graders benefit from a lower student-teacher ratio in the afternoon when the kindergarteners go home.

At the Leonard Johnson Day Nursery in Englewood, New Jersey, Donna Lee Scro leads seventeen four- and five-year-olds for eight hours a day in activities varying from math and reading readiness to art, music and science.

The needs of disadvantaged children has been dealt with successfully through transitional classes at John F. Kennedy School in Blackstone, Massachusetts. These self-contained units operate each level of grades one through six. They contain no more than fifteen youngsters, each classified as a slow learner because deprived economic and environmental backgrounds have contributed to their lack of academic success. Federal funding for this program provides for a teacher and a teacher's aide in each class. A novel element of the Kennedy school's approach to developing these youngsters' motor coordination, personal evolution development, improved self-image and self-confidence can be found in a ten-week swimming program conducted during regular school hours at the local Y.M.C.A.

Today, answers and programs for the needs of disadvantaged children are found sprouting up and thriving as a result of innovative and resourceful curriculum designs coming from all walks of life:

■ Teachers and curriculum design:
An interesting approach has been employed in the Kennedy School in Blackstone to help students who suffer from behavioral and emotional problems become accountable for their classroom

143

behavior, as well as their school work. The town's kindergartners and first- through third-graders benefit from a two-fold approach. For one, the school sends a weekly report home to the child's parents, stating the child's progress in both the learning center and the regular classroom; the parents then return the report adding their own comments. Secondly, the school has instituted an individual behavior modification program which operates jointly with the regular curriculum. The children earn points for completing work and behaving properly. Whether work completion or behavior is stressed is dependent upon each individual child's problem. At the end of the week, if a child has earned the specified number of points, he or she may choose a small prize.

The Hartwick Elementary School in Gilbertsville, Massachusetts, has developed its career education program based on a model designed for elementary schools by the Department of Health, Education and Welfare. In their version, the Hartwick teachers incorporate career education lessons into the school's social studies and language arts classes. In presenting the program, teachers employ commercially-made materials, hand-made aids, and resource people from the local community to reinforce regular classroom teaching plus home economics and physical education. The curriculum activities are planned to encourage an early development of self-awareness.

The Hartwick Elementary School has also designed a Child Study Program to help teachers focus on a child's problems, find ways of meeting the child's needs, and follow through with the solutions. This program begins with a meeting of the child's current and previous-year teachers along with the principal and anyone else with relevant information. The presence of the child's previous year's teachers enables present teachers to understand the child and the child's problems better, as well as get advice on how to handle them. These thirty-minute meetings are held either before or after school.

The Child Study meetings' format includes identification of problems through test results, papers, and such things as behavior reports; after discussion, a course of action is determined. This may consist of asking the child's parents to attend the next meeting; or a psychological support team may be asked to observe the child; or a "TEAM" meeting may be called involving a speech therapist, school psychologist, nurse, administrator, classroom teacher and a special education teacher. Finally, and perhaps most importantly, a follow-up meeting takes place in which appropriate action is discussed and specific recommendations for action are made.

In a certain part of Massachusetts there exists a special curriculum somewhat modeled after the "open-classroom" concept developed in Leicester, England, using the team-teaching concept. Here can be found a pleasant cove with a small frame school building that no longer serves the modern needs of today's school facilities. However, its nearby beach and tree-studded lots serve perfectly as a backdrop for a special summer school for children who are failing to achieve in school because of cultural deprivations, social lag, or lack of confidence.

The children arrive at the school just in time for breakfast. After breakfast, they complete remedial work in math and reading, and pursue activities in arts and crafts, nature studies, swimming, general recreation and field trips. Each team of teachers has a male and a female member in hopes that such an arrangement will give each student someone he/she can relate to more closely. The curriculum was built around a program designed to help the children gain confidence in their own abilities and thus become better students during the school year.

■ Corporations:

A pilot program for seventeen schools in Florida was developed by retired school principal, John Henry Martin, recalling his boyhood initiation into writing through chalking letters upon a slate. He calls his program "Writing To Read." The program, underwritten by IBM, uses the computer or word processor as the modern equivalent of the slate. With it, Martin's program encourages children to form letters, words and sentences on the screen and thereby enter the process of writing to read.

145

■ Parents and communities:

The Woburn Street School in Wilmington, Massachusetts, has over one hundred parents actively participating in the educational efforts of their children's school. This high degree of parental involvement has endured for the last ten years, with parents volunteering their time and talents in serving on the Parent Advisory Council, as classroom volunteers, room mothers, aides in the resource room and media center, and participating on one or more of the school's various special committees.

One subcommittee of the Parent Advisory Council publishes a handbook and quarterly newspaper and sponsors speakers who visit the school and talk about safety, fire and other pertinent subjects—all in an effort to enhance and strengthen communications among the home, the community, and the school. While many schools publish books and newsletters, Woburn Street's publications are handled totally by the parents—either writing the articles themselves or having someone in the community contributing—from typing the stencils and mimeographing the copy, to collating the pages, stapling and distributing.

The Lincoln Elementary School in South Attleboro, Massachusetts, encourages parental participation in their child's schooling through a similar successful communication technique. Every Friday each pupil takes home a large manila envelope containing samples of his or her work for the week. A newsletter, written by the teacher, is also included in the packet; it relates the class news, and gives assignments and suggestions to help the children do better in school. This practice encourages parents to sit down with their children to review the child's work, to talk about the assignments and discuss the newsletter.

And the Wrentham Public School System in Wrentham, Massachusetts, has enjoyed a strong relationship with its public sector as a result of the program they offer to parents and interested community leaders—a private tour of the entire school system.

The success of these programs is evidence that, regardless of deprivation, all children can learn. In order for them to do so,

146

however, we must be willing to create and offer eclectic opportunities for learning. We are witnessing the development of many excellent programs uniquely suited to disadvantaged children. The real problem is the swelling number of such children versus the number of such programs. These children can be rescued, as were the ones in the programs we have cited, from the world of defeat surrounding them. It will be an immense task but one we must undertake if only because its alternative is the road to national self-destruction.

APPENDIX C:

Dealing With Older Students

The counter-classroom culture now claiming so much student time, may actually re-define the fundamental nature of school itself—transforming our very idea of education over the next decade. Ernest Boyer has said: "I believe the stimulation, the distractions, the perhaps premature confidence that children and young people establish in the culture today, puts the school and the classroom on the defensive. They've acquired so much and the school, perhaps, is seen as almost a distraction in their lives. Now, that's always been true to some extent, but I think in the last ten–twenty years, that's clearly the dramatic trend. Indeed, looking ahead, the question remains: 'Will the school be the primary teacher, or will the non-formal teachers be prominent?' " And Dr. Boyer goes on to describe what he means by informal teachers: ". . . magazines, video cassettes, records, radio, travel, peers. These are the places where the sources of knowledge increasingly are for our children. The question is: will the school become increasingly dreary and obsolete and the young people feel more and more alienated in this process, while they rely more and more on the informal teachers beyond the classroom, that they depend on because they're spending more time with them?" However, it is possible the schools have another choice. If, as Marshall McLuhan remarked, "The medium is the message,'' then educators can utilize these so-called distractions as a bridge to guide young people back to traditional educational values.

Just such a problem confronted Rutgers University in Newark, New Jersey, in 1978, when I went there to teach writing and intensive composition courses. A large body of students—in great part minority and immigrants, but also disadvantaged students from other backgrounds—were entering the university because of open admissions. In many cases, their writing skills, although bolstered by as many as four remedial classes, were barely acceptable. Although they often knew the rules of grammar, these rules were suspended, except for filling in sentences and picking out the right multiple-choice answer on tests. Many students could not write a literate paragraph, much less a formal composition.

In order to deal with their intense problems, I used a new method called Kaleidoscopic Composition. Accepting that virtually instantaneous communication is a daily part of young people's lives, I was led to the recognition that media could be a significant educational tool to help students comprehend, utilize and write about complex ideas.

This method, Kaleidoscopic Composition, has both grammar and reading components. It is based on a series of sources: contemporary non-fiction essays and articles, literature, non-print media, music, art, film, and materials from the popular culture. These materials are organized into a series of thematic lessons which focus upon an issue, concern of topic: teenage suicide, drugs, heroism, sports and male and female liberation, to name a few examples. All issues are related to major concerns of today's students (as verified by outside researchers). The student is made aware that all these works are chosen for their relevance; he or she is then faced with the necessity of ascertaining how the central issues in a particular piece pertains to the ideas under discussion. Thus, each essay, short story, record, advertisement or poem may be viewed in the light of other considerations, and is no longer remote from the student's interest or understanding.

Grammar is broken up into a series of progressive blocks

known as Color Language. During the first coloring session, major deficiencies—such as finding central issues, tense fluctuations and point of view—are taken up. As the course progresses, smaller blocks of problems are confronted and solved. The movement is from the composition as a whole, to the paragraph, sentence and words. In this way, major problems are worked on first and, as the student corrects and becomes encouraged by his or her improvement in solving these areas, smaller problems are tackled. We were able—through this Kaleidiscopic method—to decrease the percentage of students in intensive composition sections failing the interdepartmental final from 20 percent to 1 percent, and this figure remained stable for the five-year period during which the pilot testing of the method took place. The pilot plan has since been adapted for high school use.

An example of a test lesson on the theme identity is described by Rutgers professor Virginia Hyman: "The class was well-attended and began promptly, with Dr. Dunphy using as her introduction the quotation from James Baldwin, which she had written on the board: 'I try to write as jazz musicians sound to reflect their compassion.'

"The instructor's goal was to show the way in which the arts express similar values and reveal similar techniques. Since today's students are more familiar with the themes and techniques of music than with those of literature, Dr. Dunphy used that familiarity as the bridge into greater familiarity and understanding of literary techniques.

"She began by playing tapes of the kinds of music referred to in the Baldwin story under consideration: 'Blues for Mr. Charley.' Moving to the text, she asked students to identify the allusions to music and to explain their significance. In each case her questions moved from those of simple identification to those requiring more careful analysis, and finally to questions involving more subtle inferences. She called on a wide range of students, who, for the most part, responded well.

"By the end of the class, the instructor had effectively demonstrated the similarity between the effects of the story (its shifts

of tone and mood, and its contrapuntal movement) and the techniques of the kind of music Baldwin was imitating. The lesson
ended with Dr. Dunphy's returning to the quotation she had cited
initially, and with the announcement of the class's next assign-
ment. They were to write about the theme of music in the Baldwin
story in the next class.''

And in other schools—at every level of learning—similarly
successful innovations in curriculum and methodology attacking
the problems pinpointed as critical to achieving a major turna-
round in both the quantity and quality of American education are
being tried:

- The Joseph G. Pyne School in Lowell, Massachusetts, is
  implementing an alternative play for remedial instruction.
  Here teachers identify potential remedial students and, on
  a voluntary basis, give them the extra help they need during
  the course of the regular school day when they are not
  scheduled in academic classes. The objective at the Pyne
  School is to individualize seventh- and eighth-grade remedial programs—limiting each group to no more than three
  students. In addition, a trained counselor also offers individual counseling both during and after school hours as
  needed.

Another method of learning being introduced because of the
media-induced short attention span of older students today, is an
innovative program called "Walkabout!" The philosophy upon
which this curriculum is based was articulated by Maurice Gib-
bons, who suggested that we need to provide our adolescents
with a transition into adulthood through growing achievements
in a range of adult skills. Using this concept, several schools
have developed alternative non-traditional programs for those
students whose personal or educational needs were not being met
through traditional patterns of schooling:

- In one such school, Jefferson Country Open High School

in Evergreen, Colorado, three examples illustrate the "Walkabout" program: the first is Community Learning—a program of apprenticeships; the second is Operation Sundance—a program in which students learn about alternative forms of energy by designing and building a solar greenhouse; and the third is Munchie Central—a student-designed and created school cafeteria which has served as a deterrent to absenteeism during and after the lunch hour.

- Another creative program has been undertaken by the high school in Yorktown, New York. This "Walkabout" has been so successful that the school has received grants to replicate the system in other schools. To this end, educators prepare day-long seminars on personal effectiveness for teachers and administrators. Seminars called I.D.E.A. have been given to twenty-five schools in the Yorktown region in the last three-and-a-half years in an effort to help prepare students for adulthood and to make use of the latest concepts in organizational effectiveness and seminars on parenting strategy are used to help counsel parents on helping adolescents deal with problems of self-esteem, responsibility, and motivation. The program has been called one of the top forty experimental programs in the United States.

- At New Garden Friends School—a small alternative school sponsored by the Quakers in Greensboro, North Carolina—the 1983-1984 school year marked the beginning of the upper school program. The school has tried to develop a program of individual learning, using the community as a learning resource. Upper school students spend the mornings working on traditional academic subjects, and the afternoons are devoted to Challenge Education. Each semester, students choose one structured group challenge and one independent challenge designed and contracted by the student. The challenges are quite varied: one student has been learning auto mechanics by taking apart an engine and putting it back together; another is serving as an intern with a park ranger; and still another student has been studying dying by en-

152

rolling in a hospice training course. A wide range of students attend the school, some because their parents appreciate Quaker values and others because of learning disabilities and lack of motivation.

- In an attempt to fill a particular void existing in the education of many of today's adolescents, the Peter Thacher Middle School's Parents Association in Attleboro, Massachusetts, has introduced a curriculum design called "Personal Development and Human Sexuality." This program—one of very few such classes in New England—focuses on questions of preteenage students regarding their growing bodies and the difference between males and females, reproduction and childbirth, and the role heredity plays in shaping individual's lives.
- At Winter High School in Winter Park, Florida, the atmosphere is enlivened by props bringing visual stimuli into the education experience: A chariot sits parked in the school lot, clowns in acrobatic postures move about the computer room, and a WWI soldier pops into a classroom. The clowns are really math teachers, the Latin class built the chariot, and the WWI soldier is the chairman of a department. Whatever the subject matter, the teachers at this school strive to make each topic as practical and relevant as possible. There are curricula offerings for the gifted, the academically handicapped, and the average student. Courses at Winter Park High reflect the diversity of the twenty-one hundred students of every ethnic, racial and socioeconomic background. Many of the students live in the area, but others are bused in. Almost all the students seem to function well in the lively environment, with 75 percent of them going on to four-year colleges, 17 percent to two-year colleges, and 2 percent to trade schools. In 1983, Winter Park had ten National Merit semi-finalists—more than any other public high school in Florida.
- The concept of a "magnet" school—with students of various racial and cultural backgrounds from all areas of the

surrounding community attending—is found to be an effective alternative in West Roxbury, Massachusetts, at the Dr. Wm. H. Ohrenberger School. Here, a parent-helper program was initiated to involve parents, particularly minority parents, in school activities and thus improve home-school relationships. A screening committee of two teachers and one parent interviews all interested candidates, offering incentive pay for their efforts. This tutorial teacher-aide program asks parents to tutor children who have been absent from school, to help the teacher with clerical jobs, and overall, free the teacher to devote more time to lesson planning. In addition, local college students also assist in the program, being given a small stipend for correcting papers, and tutoring small groups and invididual children, Many, studying to become teachers themselves, welcome the opportunity to participate in such an apprenticeship.

- The most cost-efficient way to raise student achievement scores is peer tutoring, according to researchers Henry Levin, Gene Glass and Gail Meister of the Institute of Research on Educational Finance and Governance at Stanford University. This type of instruction provides a better return on the school dollar than computer-assisted instruction, smaller class size or increased learning time. When money is limited, this type of instruction provides almost four times as large an effect on reading and math scores. It is a valuable tool for reform in our cost-conscious era.

School teams war on drug addiction through various recent programs:

- For fighting substance abuse our best weapons are in the hands of those closest to students: parents, peers, school officials, and health care professionals. The Federal drug abuse education and prevention strategy is now centered on helping these individuals be more effective in their fight to keep drugs out of the classroom. Twenty-five hundred teams of parents, school officials, and community leaders have been trained in the last ten years to solve public school drug problems. In the first six months of 1982, over eighty thousand volunteer hours were mobilized in local communities. These teams are often more effective than individuals. Through the school-team approach, the department joins with individuals and public and private organizations to aid school in providing a drug-free environment for learning.

- To educate pupils and parents on drug abuse—as well as the metric system and typing—the Lewis Elementary School in Everett, Massachusetts, offers after-school mini-courses for Lewis students, their parents and local high school students.

- Through the united efforts of faculty and administration at the Brookline High School in Brookline, Massachusetts, an interdisciplinary approach to the problem of alcohol abuse has been implemented. While the initial impetus for such a program arose from the teachers' need for training in dealing with this illness, it has blossomed into an all-encompassing approach—including students trained to serve as peer educators, moderating group discussions and making presentations to various classes. As a result, a group of dedicated and informed professionals have materialized from these young students—improvising their own audio-visual aids and carrying their expertise before the public through alcohol abuse presentations.

- Finally, the application of brainstorming sessions coupled with a special service referred to as the "Alternative Room," have proved successful at the Easton Junior High School in North Easton, Massachusetts. Brainstorming sessions are held in an effort to stave off possible future difficulties within the school, and are attended by the guidance staff, the resource teacher, the school nurse and concerned faculty members. When particular students are identified as exhibiting emotional disabilities, The Alternative Room is there to offer a quiet, relaxed atmosphere where these problems can be discussed with a professional. Here the students are shown ways to improve their self-image, learn appropriate socialization skills and, thus, improve their academic performance.

New disciplinary measures, already supported by parents and teachers across the United States, are being instituted by schools which must cope with the serious problem of disruptive students. Examples:

- The Leon D. Brandeis School on Manhattan's Upper West Side has an enrollment of thirty-six hundred students—all from poor minority families living in West Harlem. The attendance level—around 79 percent—is above the New York City average. And although the drop-out rate unfortunately remains firmly at an astounding 50 percent, Brandeis's academic success amidst so many obstacles is often attributed to its principal, Murray Cohen, whose philosophy of cleanliness, order, traditional studies, homework and achievement is in evidence. Underlying Brandeis's educational code is a disciplinary one which demands that students behave themselves in school—and despite the presence of gang members, etc., for the most part, they do. Separate classes have been established for 221 students who require individual attention, and an inordinate amount of discipline; among them are seventy-one neurologically impaired students. Discipline is firmly and impartially administered, yet the school tries to make discipline as mild—and above all, as personal—as possible. Serious offenses, such as carrying a weapon, call for automatic suspension and possible criminal proceedings. During 1984 there were no such cases.
- At Forsyth-Satellite Academy—a New York City alternative public high school—students create, monitor and enforce conduct standards. Ninety percent of the school's student population were truant and drop-outs. Yet, at Satellite their attendance is between 80 and 85 percent now. After five

156

years, the incidence of violent attacks against staff members is zero. There have been only a few isolated cases of theft and violence of one student against another, and no vandalism. What makes Satellite work is student participation in three areas: student intake, peer counseling and discipline. Students sit on the enrollment committee, counsel newcomers through Family Group sessions, and sit on the discipline committee. Under this system, students and staff collaborate to create a safe, effective learning environment.

According to the September 1, 1985 issue of the New York Times, on Long Island, in Westchester and Rockland Counties in southwestern Connecticut and northern New Jersey, parents want the schools to search students for drugs, discipline them for drinking and instruct teenagers about sexuality. In response to family demands many schools have or are considering enlarging their programs to cope with drug and alcohol abuse.

A Supreme Court decision earlier in 1985 in New Jersey has made it easier for school officials to search students and their desks or lockers but the Civil Liberties Union as well as other private attorneys see such actions as contrary to individual rights. One school in East Rutherford, New Jersey, ordered annual drug tests for all students in high school but found the proposal blocked by a judge.

During the spring of this past year, a high school principal in Plymouth, Connecticut, ordered a search of 130 seniors on a class picnic after three students were discovered to be carrying alcohol. Although this particular procedure met with mixed reactions from students and parents, there is a new policy in Plymouth which is being studied as a model for other schools in the state that school officials may make ''reasonable searches of a particular student and school property when there is reasonalbe cause to believe that that student may be in the possession of drugs, weapons, alcohol and other material in violation of school policy or state law.'' More intrusive searches, however, cannot be conducted without calling the students' parents and getting police officers to make the actual search.

157

These new demands by parents that schools cope with social as well as academic problems in the schools creates a number of new issues about the schools' responsibilities for dealing with and curing society's problems as well as being responsible for educating the young.

Although authority-imposed discipline is one answer to chronic school violence, the real solution must center on students themselves. They can be the most powerful motivators for change. As once dissident young people gradually develop self-disciplining skills—which means as they are encouraged and aided to do so—they increasingly assume guidance roles formerly performed by teachers, counselors and parents. This self-regulation makes it possible for once-dissident students to achieve their maximum educational potential and human development.

The problem of school drop-outs is all too familiar and calls for a major effort on the part of educators to find methods of winning back lost students:

- The Oxford, Massachusettts Public School system is fighting this crisis in education. The Cooperative Federation for Educational Experience—known as C.O.F.F.E.E.—is an alternative occupational education program for alienated secondary school students, which began in 1979. During this time the program has grown from three participating schools to nine with a waiting list. One-hundred-thirty-five students have gone through the program; only five did not graduate from high school.

  Project C.O.F.F.E.E. offers a good example of the meaningful contribution that can be made to public education through the careful orchestration of industry, school system, state and local social service agencies. At Oxford, Digital Equipment Corporations's (DC) Educational Services has underwritten C.O.F.F.E.E.'s Computer Center Digital's commitment to high-tech has helped Oxford's students increase their skills in computer and electronic literacy from 1 percent to 65 percent.

C.O.F.F.E.E.'s approach is four-fold: basic skills instruction, occupational training, individual and group counseling, and physical education. And the hands-on occupational program involves five different programs: (1) Data processing, which includes training as a computer operator, programmer, service technician, and data entry operator; (2) Electronic assembly training in layout, manufacture, and assembly of printed circuit boards with electronic components; (3) Building and grounds maintenance, offering experience in carpentry, plumbing, electrical wiring, painting, and landscaping—emphasizing state-of-the-art technologies such as energy conservation and conversion techniques and solar power; (4) Horticulture/Agriculture, where students operate a solar greenhouse and a small farm; and (5) Distributive Education, with students managing and operating a customized silk-screening/printing service. Oxford's C.O.F.F.E.E. program truly shows how schools, local businesses and social service agencies can work together to make learning meaningful for disillusioned students.

Some other innovative programs for those students who are on the verge of dropping out of school are the Educational Collaborative for Greater Boston Inc., called EdCo by its trainees. The program offers teenagers job training and remedial education. Other solutions to lowering the hazardous waste of future minds are:

- Job Corps which puts teenagers into live-in centers and gives them a basic education. It now serves sixty thousand youths.
- Job Start is being tested at ten locations and is similiar to Job Corps but youths live at home and attend alternative schools.
- Job Entitlement—a major program in 1978-1980 but now limited to a handful of cities due to government budget cuts, gives teenagers full-time minimum-wage jobs in the summer and part-time employment during school if they meet academic standards.

Another initiative for ending the problem of youths leaving school before graduating has come from the President of the National Educational Association, Mary Futrell recently announced a national campaign to keep children from dropping out of school She will take one dollar in dues from each of the N.E.A.'s members for program grants and an endowment. The N.E.A. hopes the $700,000 in grants in 1985-86 and the prospect of a one million dollar endowment will inspire teachers to think of imaginative ways to keep youngsters in school. Promising programs are likely to emphasize student's self-esteem, closer adult supervision, access to social services and more flexible curriculum and class schedules. Since children often begin drifting off at an early age, many need special reinforcement in the early and middle grades. And we must find further solutions. Although there are examples of effective drop-out programs which have exciting potential—alternative and magnet school programs have shown promise with this problem—they are only a beginning. Harold Howe II of the Harvard Graduate School of Education has said: "If a hospital managed to kill off 40 percent of its patients, it would make headlines."

School failures may be attributed to emotional problems, lack of motivation, outside work, lack of adequate goals, belief that there is a lack of relevancy of the school in further career and vocational goals, as well as financial shortages. However, to find solutions, schools must survey their own deficiencies and find ways to bring back this huge group of former students.

But, special programs are required to entice students who left school to return. Relevant entrance procedures, counseling, educational supports, a faculty attuned to interaction among themselves and students prior to and after registration are necessities. New ways to appraise what a student brings to school in the way of interests and abilities must be found. When a student drops out of school, usually neither the institution nor the student is benefited. Schools across the United States must find a way to bring their lost sheep home.

Although racial schism is a major school problem, there are

some schools that are racially and socioeconomically integrated, and, they work. These schools have demanding curricula, trained teachers, and eager students, most of whom go on to higher education. They are among the most outstanding schools in the nation. Among these in New York are Peter Stuyvesant High School in Lower Manhattan, Brooklyn Tech in the Fort Green section of Brooklyn, the School of the Performing Arts in New York's mid-town theatre district, Aviation High School in Queens, Bronx High School of Science, and Edward R. Murrow High School in Brooklyn. Each of these schools is selective in terms of the student body and faculty. For instance, Stuyvesant requires a city-wide entrance exam and at Brooklyn Tech more students take physics—about twenty-two hundred yearly—than in the public schools of most entire states.

Finally, perhaps some significant solutions for the problems of disadvantaged children may be found in the following success stories, where schools across the country have taken the lively mix of economic, cultural and racial backgrounds in designing new, innovative and—most important—successful curricula:

- The Dr. Wm. H. Ohrenberger School in West Roxbury, Massachusetts, drawing its students from all races, promotes a multi-cultural theme. Children are taught to understand children of different cultures, with the teachers using their own materials as well as those sold by commerical publishing houses to accomplish this goal. The school's multi-cultural advisory committee is composed of teachers, parents, a coordinator, and a part-time college consultant. All work together in planning and executing a curriculum which will succeed in enhancing the children's self-awareness and awareness of others.
- John Ericsson Junior High School in Brooklyn, New York, provides scheduling that balances the advantages of homogeneous and heterogeneous grouping for its student body composed of nearly 50 percent Hispanics—in total nearly 70 percent minority. The vast majority comes from low-

income homes. Students are placed in high- medium- and low- achievement groupings in English, math, social studies, and science, according to their combined scores on achievement tests in reading and mathematics. All classes are then scheduled at the same time for a given subject. Within each ability level, students are assigned heterogeneously, affording each class a substantial range of abilities. This arrangement makes it possible to reassign students from class to class within their level without introducing very wide extremes in achievement. It also facilitates scheduling of teacher and staff planning sessions, focusing on effective delivery instruction to students at a particular level of achievement.

Following Ericsson's lead, there is now a city-wide emphasis to reduce pullouts. Except for one special education teacher who works several periods a day with very small groups of "disabled" students and non-readers, pullout arrangements have been eliminated in reading and math. Instead, teachers funded by Chapter 1, by the state of New York, and by other special funds for disadvantaged students work with youngsters in small "parallel" classes for low-achievers. And the results? In 1972 median reading achievement at Ericsson was at the 20th percentile. However, reading scores have increased regularly since then, with 58 percent of the students reading at or above grade level in 1983.

- When San Jose, California's LeyVa's Junior High School opened back in 1976, a bouquet of Asian and Black, Hispanic and Anglo Saxon sixth through eighth-graders swept through the doors of its two main buildings, mired in a sea of mud and community indifference. But LeyVa's teachers and principal were determined to make their new school work. With an enrollment of students who saw no reason to respect learning, one another or themselves, these dedicated professionals had their work cut out for them, many were ready to quit after a year or two.

Yet many of the original teachers are still at LeyVa. The

buildings are surrounded by lawns and sports fields, students are strongly attached to their teachers and their school, and parents come to school frequently to take part in advisory groups, tour the school, or get child-rearing tips. One seasoned eighth-reader even confesses that ''science is still fun, even though it's not elective any more.'' Every student takes three years of English, math, and social studies, two years of science. French and Spanish are among the electives.

LeyVa's success story is a testimonial to the importance of combining determination, imagination, and dedication to our country's school systems from every segment of our great society: a determined, innovative and cohesive staff of teachers and administrators which, by trying new approaches and perfecting old ones, encouraged the students to take an interest in learning and in themselves; a state grant, guided by English teacher Sarah McCall, funded projects to build self-esteem; the community, in turn, began to take pride in the school; and when students realized that their parents *and* teachers were united, their own commitment grew; classes were developed to match every level of current ability—in English and math, for example from Gifted and Talented Education to compensatory labs funded by Chapter 1, the federal program for disadvantaged students; students have learned, too, to appropriate LeyVa's economic, cultural and racial diversity, with a student body of about 35 percent Hispanic, 33 percent Anglo, 20 percent Black and 12 percent Asian, speaking fourteen languages, and 7 percent speaking little or no English.

We must not wring our hands and write off a large portion of our young students because they are different or dissidents. If students do not respond to existing educational environment, then the initiative to resensitize the students will have to come from the schools. Boyer points out that schools are set up to serve young people, but the young don't feel the schools belong to them. The pervasive torpor in many classrooms is often the result of students feeling that what is being taught is not part of their world, not—in the cliche of the sixties—relevant. We can not wait for them to look back later and regret what they have missed. Harold Howe II, former U.S. Commissioner of Education, has described contemporary American youth as "an island in our society." If so, we must create the bridges now to link their culture to the mainland of sound education they shall need to become responsible members of their own communities and our world.

APPENDIX D:

Restoring Teacher Confidence and Competence

The basis for quality learning is quality teaching, but as most of us are aware, many of our teachers are demoralized by low salaries, low esteem and indifferent students. There is no doubt that in order to reach the level of academic excellence America needs for economic and social well-being, fundamental reforms must be instituted in our educational system: teachers' salaries should be raised; standards should be raised; liberal scholarships offered and incompetents fired or retrained. The Catch-22 is how to achieve such goals here and now—when we have supported legislators who have cut federal and state expenditures for public education; when talented people don't enter teaching because of low salaries; when the state of most of our nation's teaching programs is desperate and good teachers are leaving the class-rooms—either burned out or looking for better jobs.

It is clear that immediate teacher-aid requires more than a

knowledge of what needs to be changed. We have this and yet the quality of our teaching force is rapidly deteriorating. What is needed is a clear sense of what can be accomplished today within the constraints of social and economic policies now in effect. By placing immediate policies of change within the context of long-term goals, we can begin to halt the decay and affect real reformation in the teaching profession.

Many state legislatures have or will consider significant school reforms during their sessions:

- And at the lead of this crusade stands Tennessee's Comprehensive Education Reform Act of 1984, with over $400 million earmarked for the 1984-85 school year, to be followed by $1 billion over the following three years. Holding the much-applauded distinction of being the first of all-encompassing career incentive pay system for teachers in America, this program focuses upon improving the skills of public school teachers, providing advancement within teaching, and increasing all teachers' salaries by 10 percent. The new plan provides for special pay supplements: for undergraduate student teachers in an effort to entice more men and women to choose teaching as their career, and for the top three steps of a five-stage career ladder, the incentives for the latter ranging from one to seven thousand dollars. To help lessen the burden of overworked teachers, a program costing $6.5 million in 1984-85 was provided for teacher aides in the lower grades. Finally, the introduction of more rigorous standards to restore fine quality teachers to the classrooms includes increasing eligibility for tenure from three to four years, introducing more demanding course requirements for undergraduates, requiring such teaching institutions to be held accountable in producing graduates who can achieve a 70 percent passing rate on the state teacher examination or face probation, and implementing more rigorous teacher evaluations at the state and local levels.

Similarly, legislators in Washington have begun to take positive steps in school reform:

- In March of 1984, Congress enacted Sub. H.B. 1246—a reform law requiring "goal-setting" involving educators, community and business leaders, and citizens. Monies available to each school district are to be accounted for, insuring that "economics in management and operation" are assured. Student attainment in each district will function as a barometer for that district's learning objectives, with the entire process to receive review and evaluation at least once every two years.

In addition, part of this emergency action for a revitalization of teachers must come from within the profession itself. This response has begun:

- At the National Education Association meeting in June 1985, two resolutions—one endorsing tests as part of the assessment of new teachers, and the other backing the dismissal of experienced teachers judged to be incompetent—were approved by the seventy-five hundred teachers who represent 1.7 million members of the association.
- Albert Shanker, the President of the American Federation of Teachers, whose membership is six hundred thousnd, has already announced that he supports national examinations for new teachers.

These two measures are examples of the new initiative by teachers to halt the drift toward mediocrity and incompetence threatening their profession. Other members of the teaching profession are also answering the call for reform:

- Leading professional journals indicate the massive, new research being conducted on the teaching profession into areas of concern such as curriculum content, revised teacher education, leadership, and fiscal support.

- The Commission on Teacher Education has been created by leaders of the nation's schools of education.
- At Harvard's Principal Center, five hundred principals are designing their own systems for professional growth.
- Another way in which educators are answering their own needs is by upgrading teacher standards by revitalizing teacher-training programs at their own institutions. PRO-TEACH—short for professional teacher—an experimental program for preservice teacher preparation at the University of Florida, is a good example of such revitalized policies.

The College of Education at the University has once again demonstrated its commitment to state-of-the-art teacher training by redesigning its curriculum to include more courses in professional education, more study in the existing academic classes, and more clinical/classroom field work. Successful completion of this new five-year program confers the graduate with both bachelor's and master's degrees, as well as initial teacher certification. However, PRO-TEACH's unique approach is such that all five years are designed to be completed as one cohesive progression of academics and professional service training—unlike the typical four-year baccalaureate followed by the one-year master's degree.

Required courses are: philosophical and social history of education, human development, learning and cognition in education, mainstreaming of handicapped students, educational diagnosis and evaluation, and educational media. For those preparing to teach elementary school where a broad range of subject knowledge is required, additional courses are required in interpersonal relations/parenting and computer instruction, and the candidate must add at least one academic specialization in one of the departments of the College of Liberal Arts and Sciences.

The completion of the special education program affords

the student certification to teach two of the following four specializations: emotionally handicapped, physically hand-icapped, mentally retarded, or learning disabled. Eighteen hours in one related academic specialization outside of the College of Education is also a requirement.

Finally, a secondary education majors must complete the baccalaureate program in the College of Liberal Arts and Sciences, while also taking a minimum of thirteen credit hours in education. A concentration of indepth, "institution-like" activities are introduced in the fifth year, culminating with each individual's training being finely-honed through team-teaching experiences.

The entire PROTEACH program—designed by today's teachers for tomorrow's—offers an excellent foundation upon which to build excellence in teacher education for teacher-training schools across the country.

● Likewise, responding to a challenge made by the American Association of Colleges for Teacher Education (AACTE) in 1976, the University of Kansas has augmented its teacher-training curriculum from four to five years. The AACTE's Bicentennial report entitled *Educating a Profession,* implored teacher educators to "take bold steps to help raise teaching from the ranks of the semi-professions." This call has been earnestly undertaken at the School of Education and, to date, the results are heartening.

● The Fall of 1983 saw the Oregon State University/Western Oregon State College (OSU/WOSC) heralding a "warranty assurance" program developed by its School of Education. This commitment introduces a pledge of "quality assur-ance" by teacher-training institutions—an agreement to being held accountable for the achievements, or lack thereof, of their graduates. Under this program, the failure of a graduate to perform adequately in the classroom carries with it the guarantee that the teacher's alma mater will provide assistance and support to the employing school and retraining to the teacher in question. This plan, as well as the introduction of a national standard for such a warranty, has been endorsed by the AACTE. Provisions for the program involve four steps: (1) classroom observations by building principals three times each year, (2) evaluation of performance, (3) development of a "plan of assistance" designed to improve a teacher's less-than-satisfactory performance. The execution of the fourth step, and perhaps most important, is where the OSU/WOSC School of Education would step in to provide for consultant services to both the principal and teacher, and additional education courses for the beginning teacher—*at no cost to the school district or teacher!*

While the School of Education is able to fund basic follow-up services under such a program, it appears obvious that additional monies from business and industry, communities, and public schools are needed for continued success. Three such coalitions already in operation are: the Action Alliance for Excellence in Education which reviews educational reform proposals and either funds them directly or raises funds from other sources; the Orgeon Alliance for Program Improvement, dedicated to staff development and the establishment of integrated programming to enhance adult and vocational education; and the Valley Education Consortium, which is actively redesigning student assessment and curriculum development through the creative use of a data bank.

Many authorities feel if the quality of education is to improve, teachers must be regularly further trained and recertified in their subject areas. And by the end of 1985, as many as forty states will require some form of recertification for in-service teachers

- Numerous educational experts think that teachers should be recertified to insure their continued growth in knowledge and competency. And among the revolutionary approaches to recertification requirements is Greenville, South Carolina's pilot model for district-planned recertification. Prior to its inception in early 1982, the old recertification program simply required teachers to complete six semester hours of additional college academics every five years. The new plan, however, enables teachers to accumulate 120 renewal points within that same time frame for their active participation in district developmental activities. Such a combination of academic stimulation and field work would begin to better serve the instructional needs for both teachers and pupils. Greenville's program is awaiting approval by South Carolina's Department of Education.

Similar point-system-based recertification plans are presently in use in North Carolina, Georgia, and Florida, while the practice of issuing lifetime teacher licenses is rapidly becoming extinct. This new trend of district-planned recertification is snowballing, with twenty-nine of the forty states requiring recertification now allowing district-sponsored inservice training to qualify some of the requirements.

- Yale University, through its Yale-New Haven Teachers Institute, has offered some type of retraining to 40 percent of New Haven's middle and high school teachers. Although the budget of this university program is only $375,000, faculty members cooperate on a volunteer basis to assist in the retraining.

- The recognition—long overdue—by state governments, city councils, parent groups and the general public, that America is about to face a critical teacher shortage that promises to get worse, has caused programs and initiatives to solve the dual problems of unstaffed classrooms and too few teacher candidates: Florida and Texas are trying to meet their immediate needs by granting alternative certification to college graduates without formal teacher training. Recruiters are traveling across America and to foreign countries such as Ireland to find new teachers. More importantly, some states and cities are offering added inducements to prospective teachers: Florida is giving four-thousand dollar yearly scholarships to college students in return for each year of teaching

171

in subjects where there is a shortage: New York is offering three-thousand dollar college scholarships and graduate fellowships as well. Houston will pay up to $32,000 in added salary to teachers who will teach bilingual education and California is considering creating a new school for master teachers and funding ''key'' schools where special funds will endow teachers and administrators developing education materials and techniques to meet future needs in our schools.

Since not all of teachers' main concerns require large expenditures nor long-term goals, they can be enacted now. Other concerns of teachers involve reallocating time and freedom to control decisions which primarily involve the teacher and his or her students. For example:

- Overloaded scheduling allows no time for teachers to observe their classrooms and teaching procedures.
- The age-old practice of teachers critiquing students' composition papers on their own time continues, due to inadequate time being provided for such responsibilities during regular school hours.
- The lack of individualized instruction for students continues, due to lack of time and over-populated classrooms.
- There exist very few opportunities for teachers to interface with other teachers, administrators and staff, again due to pressing schedules.
- Grossly abbreviated parent-teacher conferences prevail, because there are too many students to be assessed and too little time in which to do it properly.
- The shortages of classroom texts force students to share books at school, not being able to study them regularly at home.
- Arbitrary decision-making, frequently having no sound basis in practical classroom application, is often levied upon teachers.

The solutions to many of these problems can begin if student-teacher ratios can be lowered and somehow more time can be afforded to teachers during the school day, allowing for lesson planning, grading of papers and individualized instruction to be performed during regular school hours. Among the ideas being proposed to deal with these critical issues for teachers are:

- The Musconomet Regional School District in Massachusettts is considering scheduling its courses as intensive, thirty-day blocks of time, so that teachers and students would work on one subject at a time. This total-immersion theory of education would result in each teacher having a single class of about twenty-five students in each thirty-day segment.
- To instill new respect for teachers, Council Bluffs, Iowa, celebrates Teachers Day on May 6, and retailers who have been visited earlier by a "teacher recognition task force" give discounts to teachers that day. Such movements reassert public and teacher pride in teacher performance.
- To handle the problem of inadequate and unaffordable housing for teachers, some school districts in Oregon have begun imitating the practice of several universities, such as Columbia, which is a landlord with fifteen hundred apartments close to the school for faculty and staff, and New York University which has a number of low rent apartments.
- In order to develop parent-teacher relationships, a new initiative is being mounted by faculty members to increase the participation of parent organizations in the schools. Recently, the National Parent Teachers Association announced an increase of seventy-thousand members throughout the 1983 school year. During the preceding twenty years, membership in the organization had steadily declined.

Most important are developing programs to make schools safe. Both the public and teachers themselves are vitally concerned with having safe schools operating on defined codes of discipline, so that teachers can teach and students can learn without fear. Strong, aggressive measures to deal with violence have begun to be instituted by law enforcement agencies, legislators and educators, whose schools and personnel have been victims of vandalism, thefts and muggings:

- In New York, the public schools have experienced an impressive drop in crime; the teachers union credits better security for the decrease. During 1984, the number of violent incidents involving school officials dropped 18 percent, and only sixty schools out of more than a thousand accounted for the incidents. Only one school in Manhattan is rated chronically unsafe for teachers. Drops in school crime are being recorded in Chicago, Dade County, Florida, and schools near Los Angeles, where assertive new disciplinary measures are being used to combat crime.

Meanwhile, several schools have developed plans to deal with disciplinary problems themselves. For example:

- Charleston, South Carolina schools give special attention—such as tutorial assistance and psychological counseling—to students who are chronic discipline problems. Each student has access to a concerned adult who can help solve his or her problem.
- Another technique for solving disciplinary problems is being used by nearly a quarter of the nation's 2.1 million teachers who have been trained in assertive discipline so that they can confidently regain control of their classrooms.

Finally, the long-term goal of raising teachers' salaries to higher base-pay commensurate with pay scales for other professions is meritorious. But while we can lobby for such future legislation and the raised taxes it will surely require, we must not wait for these visionary provisions to come to pass while the best teachers depart, fewer and less-able candidates enter the field, and those who remain become disheartened and burned out.

174

Certain measures can be enacted now—such as salary incentives which will reduce the steps on salary scales to encourage career teachers to remain in the profession, master teacher programs, career ladders as seen in Charlotte-Mecklenburg, and merit pay as exercised in Dalton, Georgia. By programs such as these and the others, we can begin to work on one of the most pressing problems our schools face: how to attract and keep good teachers.

- The application of merit pay systems—long-utilized in the corporate world as a productive incentive program—has enjoyed twenty years of success in the Dalton, Georgia public schools. Here, the state's Department of Education establishes base-level salaries in accordance with academic degrees and post-graduate study. Then, local public school funds are tapped for merit pay incentives. Performance is evaluated by the teacher's principal (certified by the state as a classroom evaluator), reviewed by the superintendent, and, those receiving superior ratings are awarded merit pay raises of as much as three thousand dollars.
- The wealthy school system of Ledue, Missouri, has successfully utilized a merit pay system for over thirty years. This achievement is attributed to pay incentives substantial enough to induce improved performance and an evaluation system that employs fairness and a criteria mutually acceptable by teachers and administrators alike. Teachers can earn up to 15 points (each point worth three hundred dollars) based upon their evaluation in several categories, including their performance in interpersonal relations and communications, their commitment to self-improvement as demonstrated in completing continuing professional education courses on a regular basis, and their contributions to curriculum development.
  Superintendent Charles McKenna explains that while "a merit pay won't get teachers rich . . . it will give them a chance to shoot for higher goals and . . . be rewarded for

their performance,'' thus bringing stability to his teaching staffs, rather than watching bright teachers become disillusioned and stagnant, opting to change their professions.

- In Lake Forest, Illinois, the president of the school board, Frederic Genck, asserts that the basis for selection of awarding merit pay raises for teacher performance should be rooted in objective, concrete measurements of success, such as increased standardized test scores, as well as more abstract dimensions, such as parental and peer appraisals. The ''proof of the pudding'' in Lake Forest's ten-year stroke of success with the merit pay system can be found in the parents and teachers who are pleased with and proud of their schools, and standardized test scores that continue to steadily rise.

- Bruce Alexander—Round Valley, California's school board president—applied the long-standing business practice of merit pay raises for his school system of thirty-some teachers. The program was approved and implemented four years ago, with teacher performance evaluations based upon standards similar to Ledue, Missouri's mentioned earlier, as well as upon teacher-presented criteria to back up their own self-evaluations—delivered in the forms of classroom videotapes, lesson plans, and students scores on standardized tests.

  With an aggressive publicity program that regularly appraises the community of the school's successes, local taxpayers have loosened their purse strings, recognizing how well their money is being spent. Alexander notes: ''. . . now citizens know more about the good things going on in their schools,'' and similarly, he is very proud to state that ''we treat teachers like professionals, and now we pay them like professionals.''

Merit pay plans obviously provide a very real economic incentive to the underpaid, unrecognized, disillusioned classroom teacher who, increasingly, is leaving his or her chosen profession for the greater monetary rewards of business and industry. The challenge to further set into motion an appropriately-structured, unanimously-accepted merit pay system throughout our country's school system will help create successful teachers, schools, and, in the final analysis, inspired, educated, respectful and successful students.

In this last two or three years we have witnessed a flurry of reports, research studies and dooming prophecies expounding upon the deteriorating status of the American public school system. While suggested solutions are sometimes met with enthusiasm and at other times with unease, an overwhelming concensus prevails—that America's political future and economic promise critically depend upon a radical reformation of our public education system.

The increasing new wave of national and state commissions established to improve and renovate teacher education is certainly a step in the right direction. However, these politically-derived steps must progress in concert with, and in addition to, innovations by teacher educators themselves—through enhanced in-service training, as well as increased preservice training for the beginning teacher.

It's painfully clear. Teacher-training institutions *must* forcefully address themselves to the imperative need for drastic reformations in teacher education. Otherwise, if such reforms fail to take place from within our educational system, we can be assured that the unfortunate alternative will be that those forces from without will command the lead.

APPENDIX E:

Regaining Public Support

To grow and thrive, our schools must establish organic relationships with the communities of which they are integral parts. Just as "no man is an island," neither can the school remain an isolated ivory tower of learning. Miller Ritchie, former president of Hartwick College, recognized this fact when he called upon the schools to become "the community leaven"—to be part of and contribute to a wider movement than school reform: the movement to remake the common world. There is little doubt that the schools must open their doors to the communities, if the communities are to open their hearts and pocketbooks to the schools.

This open-door policy can be fostered in several ways: first, by making the activities of the schools known and participated in by a wider segment of the general public, second, by acting on what the public conceives to be crucial to school success and, finally, by initiating programs which serve community needs: Some schools have begun to reach out:

- At Leaphart Elementary School in Columbia, South Carolina, a number of procedures have been initiated by Principal George E. Pawlas and his faculty-staff, which improve public support through communication:

(1) Project LOVE—Let Older Volunteers Educate—working in concert with the Council on Aging, provides a merging of rich memories from the past with the young minds of our future. Here the volunteers share their knowledge, interests, talents, skills, and lunchtime with Leaphart's 3rd-graders one morning a week.

(2)*The Principal's Piquant Partner* is Mr. Pawlas's monthly newsletter given to each student. In an effort to keep the lines of communications open among faculty, students, parents and the community, a clip/return slip is completed and signed by parents and returned to the school—proof that classroom news has, indeed, reached home—and if more than one copy is sent to one household, parents are encouraged to pass the extra on to a neighbor or friend without children in school.

(3) The School Improvement Council—composed of parents and teachers elected to two-year terms—also includes two citizens appointed by the principal to serve as community representatives and, ultimately, as valuable liaisons in spreading positive news about the school throughout the local citizenry.

(4) The *Super Reader* program in Leaphart's version of a Read-A-Thon encouraging young students to read an assigned list of books in order to earn a Super Reader star iron-on for their Leaphart T-shirts. As each consecutive list of books is completed, new stars are added to the T-shirts. Wearing the shirts every Wednesday not only boosts school spirit, but also when the pupils wear them out and around the community local citizens get the message that Leaphart students are spending their time reading good books.

(5) An Open-Door policy encourages parents and local citizens to visit the school whenever desired—especially during American Education Week in November—for special early morning breakfasts, lunch, etc. This allows children to spend some precious time with their parents and many senior citizens within the school setting.

Staff and teachers, too, receive regular encouragement and recognition through the principal's positive notes, happy-grams and public announcements distributed from time to time to the community. Principal Pawlas is determined, along with his staff, to keep the public abreast of Leaphart's commitment to meaningful, enjoyable, quality educational opportunities being experienced by some of Columbia's children. The reason for such initiatives is clear, according to Principal Pawlas: "Almost 72 percent of American households do not have school ties; we must give them a source for positive news about the schools, the children who attend them, and their parents."

- Another method of communication is used by the Memorial in Millis, Massachusetts School and helps establish school priorities: a communications committee. This group of parents, teachers, pupils and the school's administrator face the task of establishing the school's priorities for the coming year—setting goals and working throughout the year to see to their successful completion. Some of the milestones that have been achieved by these committees in the past years have been the introduction of a sex-education curriculum for the upper-grade children, the development of an environmental/outdoor program, and the establishment of various academic clubs and intramural sports activites.

Although the general public's disenchantment with its schools have been felt for well over a decade—and seems to have been caused, in large part, by the schools' lax academic and disciplinary demands—recent opinion polls confirm that education has vaulted to the forefront of our national agenda. For example:

- In a poll taken by the Public Policy Analysis Service in the fall of 1983, over 70 percent of the respondents among all population groups across the United States agreed with the proposed dictum that the erosion of public education threatens "our future as a nation."

- A May 1983 Gallup Poll—its results further supported by two leading public opinion researchers, Robert M. Teeter and Peter Hart—indicates that American taxpayers would be willing to support increased funding for education, but only if quality can be assured.
- In October of 1983, the National Conference of State Legislatures reported that educaton—as well as crime and unemployment—ranks at the top of the Nation's domestic concerns. Unlike crime and unemployment, however, the fundamental value of education and what needs to be done to improve it saw "almost total agreement" from every diverse segment of the population.
- In a survey of important national issues in the 1984 Presidential campaign, *Newsweek* reported that education ranked second in importance to unemployment—ranking higher than the Federal deficit, inflation, protection of American jobs, and international relations with the Soviet Union.

The 1984 sixteenth annual Gallup Poll indicates that Americans are more favorably disposed toward public education than at any time during the last decade. Three important signs of this are:

- For the first time since 1976, more people rated their own school an A or B for their performance.
- A higher percentage—50 percent—graded public school teachers and administrators A or B.
- A or B grades for performance were given to 47 percent of principals.

Finally, the percentage of Americans who say they would be willing to pay more taxes for education has risen from 30 to 41 percent. However, the American public continues to feel that discipline is the most important problem facing the schools today.

In addition to problems within the school system disillusioning the public perception of school effectiveness, people are disgruntled by many schools' disinterest in solving their community's problems.

Two programs of civic support were proposed by me for universities that wished to explore becoming involved with the needs of their communities: one was the Drew Center for the Arts, the other was the C.W. Post Community for Senior Adults. The Drew Center for the Arts at Drew University in Madison, New Jersey, is a program designed to act as a leavening agent to enhance the cultural needs of its students, as well as all New Jerseyans. With the University acting as a cultural liaison through the implementation of the following programs, both the campus and community would become further enriched in the Arts and Humanities:

- Writing—Possibilities for expanding the existing curriculum would include enriched writing courses, a University Press, a journal (such as the *Sewanee Review,* etc), writing concentration in conjunction with the humanities major, an interdisciplinary major of writing and literature, and summer writers' conferences, similar to the Bread Loaf design.
- Music—Proposals include an orchestra-in-residence, a jazz institute or ensemble, ballet company, musical artist-in-residence, Annual Festival Concert, Extravaganza of the Arts (incorporating, professional theatre, dance, music, and visual art by outstanding artists from the campus and community), and utilizing New Jersey/New York dance and music groups for part-time instruction.
- Art—Artists living and working in the area would be asked to create a curriculum including museum internships, art therapy, one-day seminars, computerized art and design, illustration courses based upon the principles of fine art, community art guild affiliations, cultural art trips, summer art workshops, and an Extravaganza of the Arts—such as the one in Palm Beach, Florida—featuring demonstrations by weavers, enameling guild, painters puppetry guild, porcelain artists and exhibits of paintings, sculpture, pottery, etc.
- Theatre—Enhancement would include a modernized thea-

182

tre-in-the-round, as well as outdoor theatre facilities, an off-off Broadway alliance, including seminars by writers, producers and actors, a cooperative enterprise with the American Musical and Dramatic Academy, a choreographers' theatre dance program through the National Endowment for the Arts Dance Touring Program, and finally, an interdisciplinary theatre arts combination, to incorporate stage, film, television and speech.

A proposal for C.W. Post College on Long Island to create The C.W. Post Community for Senior Citizens, focuses upon the very real need existing among the pre-retired and retired citizenry of Long Island by providing a program offering educational, work, and social opportunities to replace those identities that recede or terminate with age. This program would take into account each individual's level of formal education and offer him/her—through a diversity of options—an opportunity for optimal self-actualization.

Six related areas which would comprise the program would include:

- (1) Pre-retirement orientation for married couples, single persons, industry and social groups;
- (2) Volunteerism and placement, calling for the development of a senior adults volunteer network at C.W. Post, using a computerized "skills pool" to match and place these senior adults in suitable positions on the campus and in the surrounding community;
- (3) Courses for senior adults would require the construction of new curricula, methods, and programs—credit and non-credit—consisting of courses on the productive use of leisure time, second careers, social and health sciences, business, and explorations in the humanities, as well as Weekend College sessions responsive to the social, intellectual and personal demands of older citizens;
- (4) Campus resources and services would involve the cus-

tomizing of the campus's facilities for cultural, recreational and social activities as needed to accommodate the Senior Adult Community, including a senior citizen's social center to function integrally with student campus life;

- (5) An evaluation program, and
- (6) A training program in gerontology.

Other schools across the country are becoming community service oriented: For instance: Yale University has donated land for Science Park, a high-technology and light industry complex that Yale is developing with the city of New Haven and the Olin Corporation. The project, which is intended to attract more than one hundred fifty businesses to the park, has already employed more than one hundred people from the disadvantaged neighborhood on the park's border. The University has also helped to renovate a downtown mall, refurbish a hotel for housing and remodel a busy downtown intersection.

The University of Rochester has joined its city's Downtown Development Corporation to develop parks and trails on both sides of the Gennesee River which runs along the main campus. Columbia University, has joined the Cathedral of St. John the Divine in planning a mixed housing project to accommodate the elderly as well as students. Trinity College plans to open a day-care center that city residents will be able to use. Such projects illustrate to local governments and residents that some schools do not have "the ivory tower" or "fortress mentality" which unfortunately discourages contact between the schools and their surrounding communities and so encourages the apathy or even hostility of the aging population. For a great deal more could and should be done unless the self-imposed isolationism of the more parochial of our institution ends, schools will be unable to create and foster the climate of support needed to cope with their critical needs.

Other avenues of contact can be opened. For instance, utilizing underenrolled school facilities for a senior citizens' center whose program might involve children and senior adults; experienced retired adults could then act as teaching resources. Other mutual programs in the fields of health, computer science, scientific laboratories, sales and marketing could be developed to create supportive relationships between the students and community members. Such programs would also aid in the vocational training of alienated students who see little connection between the schools and their own future lives.

While these programs have been proposed for implementation at institutions of higher education, similar ideas have been employed in various public schools throughout the country. In efforts to develop students' cultural interests and overall intellectual growth, individuals in local communities have generously offered their support:

- The Student Theater at the Francis W. Parker School in North Quincy, Massachusetts, encourages participation in the dramatic arts to enhance self-awareness and self-expression in an effort to help the students understand themselves and the world around them. The Parker School also sponsors "The Author Program" to foster the writing of original stories, poems and plays by the children. Each contribution is stored and referenced in a card catalogue displayed in the media center. To emphasize excellence and originality, a Francis W. Parker School certificate of excellence is awarded to a student for his/her outstanding contribution. Finally, the "Community Helpers Program" encourages the students to study their community—it's needs, problems, etc.—and then improve it in some way. Their many contributions range from beautification through planting flowers and picking up litter to providing entertainment for local nursing home residents.
- The Pine Glen Elementary School in Burlington, Massachusetts, utilizes volunteers, many are parents, to share their talents and skills during its "Creative Arts Days" throughout the school year. On these days when the school is transformed into an art festival, the children have the opportunity

to explore various artistic experiences with members of the community and faculty.

- A "Very Important People" Program (VIP) at the Leverett Elementary School in Leverett, Massachusetts, enables the students to learn from interesting adults from their community. Operating now for ten years, both the children and adults become enriched through the sharing of hobbies, interests, skills, and travel and occupational experiences.

- The Parent Advisory Council and community volunteers provide direction and support in leading "Mini-Courses" at the Osterville Elementary Schools in Osterville, Massachusetts throughout the year. The areas of interest included in this curriculum are growing plants, creative dramatics, macrame, first aid, basket weaving, and cooking, to name a few.

- The Swallow/Union School in Dunstable, Massachusetts, has found an effective means of communicating with its parents and the community by not only printing school news and upcoming events in the *King Newspaper*, but also by sending copies—which include prose and poetry written by the students—to the local newspaper and to school committee members.

- Parents and community leaders are invited to take a one-and-a-half-hour private tour of the Wrentham Public School System in Massachusetts, providing a complete introduction to all school programs in operation. This has helped the schools enjoy a strong relationship with the public sector by providing a living example of just how their tax dollars are being spent. Newspaper announcements explain the program and how to arrange tours.

- The Frederick J. Delaney School in Wrentham, Massachusetts, taps the talents and resources of its local senior citizens by asking them to help read to the kindergarten children and, in some cases, tutor some of them.

- And again, the hands of the school system reach out to the community's senior citizens at the Highland School in Fall

River, Massachusetts, where story-telling time—affectionately referred to as "The Grandmother Hour"—provides these older citizens with a useful vehicle for interacting with and contributing to the school system.

- In September of 1985, the Board of Education in New York signed a 5.65 million dollar contract with custodians that in most cases enables non-profit organizations to use the city's public schools during the afternoon free of charge. In addition, fees for school use during the summer have been cut in half. Not only community groups but youth group leaders, many fighting budget battles of their own, welcomed the new saving. It is evidence of a new, vital link between the schools and the community.

In order to preserve and restore the public's faith in education, our schools must focus not only on the larger issues but on local ones as well so that the schools' value beyond the classroom is understood and communicated. By reaching out to their communities through collaborative efforts for social and economic goals, the schools can create a new climate of public support for public education.

Source Notes

Although space limitations preclude listing all of the sources that were of value in writing this book, we use this section to document those works that are of particular importance. Unattributed quotations from the public are from personal interviews conducted for the ABC News "Closeup" documentary, "To Save Our Schools, To Save Our Children," or from Dr. Dunphy's files.

PART I: THE PERILOUS DECADE: STUDENTS

1. Bell, Terrell, former U.S. Secretary of Education under Reagan administration.

1. National Commission on Excellence in Education. *A Nation at Risk: The Imperative for Education Reform*, Washington, D.C., 1983

2. Shanker, Albert, President and Executive Director, American Federation of teachers, Washington, D.C.

3. Ravitch, Dr. Diane, Professor of Eduction, Teachers College, Columbia University, New York, N.Y.

4. Goodlad, Dr. John, Professor (Former Dean) of Education, University of California, Los Angeles, California.

5. Sizer, Theodore R., Chairperson, Department of Education, Brown University, Providence, R.I.

Chapter 1: The Children of the Dispossessed

1. Comer, Dr. James, Child Psychiatrist, Yale Medical School, Yale University, New Haven, Connecticut.

2. Goodlad, Dr. John, Professor (Former Dean) of Education, University of California, Los Angeles, California.

3. **Grand Master Flash and the Furious Five, "The Message," used with permission, Sugarhill Music Ltd., copyright 1983.**

4. Coleman, Dr. James, Professor of Education, University of Chicago, Chicago, Illinois.

5. Blanc, Dr. Robert, Professor, School of Medicine, University of Missouri, Kansas City, Missouri.

6. Boyer, Ernest L., President, Carnegie Foundation for the Advancement of Teaching, Princeton, New Jersey; Former U.S. Secretary of Education under Carter administration.

Chapter 2: The Waning of the Middle-Class Family

1. Boyer, Ernest L., President, Carnegie Foundation for the Advancement of Teaching, Princeton, New Jersey; Former U.S. Secretary of Education under Carter administration.

2. Long, Lynette, National Institute on Latch-Key Children, Glen Echo, Maryland.

3. Coles, Dr. Robert W., Professor and Child Psychiatrist, Harvard University, Cambridge, Massachusetts; Editor, *Phi Delta Kappan*.

4. Goodlad, Dr. John, Professor (Former Dean) of Education, University of California, Los Angeles, California.

Chapter 3: The Tribal World of the Young

1. Winn, Marie, author of *The Plug-In Drug: Television, Children and the Family* (New York: Pantheon Books, 1983).

2. Ravitch, Dr. Diane, Professor of Education, Teachers College, Columbia University, New York, N.Y.

3. Sykes, Gary, Professor, Stanford University, Stanford, California.

4. Boyer, Ernest L., President, Carnegie Foundation for the Advancement of Teaching, Princeton, New Jersey; Former U.S. Secretary of Education under Carter administraion.

5. Comstock, James P., Program Manager, Adolescent Care Unit, San Francisco, California.

6. National Institute on Drug Abuse, U.S. Department of Health and Human Services, Washington, D.C., 1984 survey.

7. National center for Education Statistics, U.S. Department of Education, Washington, D.C.

8. The Annual Gallup Poll on Education, Gallup Organization, Inc., Princeton, New Jersey.

9. National Education Association, Washington, D.C.

SOURCE NOTES

PART II: THE PERILOUS DECADE: TEACHERS

Chapter 4: The Imperiled Profession

1. Shanker, Albert, President and Executive Director, American Federation of Teachers, Washington, D.C.

Chapter 6: Lowered Public Esteem—Poor Pay

1. Ravitch, Dr. Diane, Professor of Education, Teachers College, Columbia University, New York, N.Y.

Chapter 7: The Places and the Players

1. Clinton, William, Governor, State of Arkansas.
2. Sixteenth Annual Gallup Poll of the Public's Attitudes Toward Schools, Gallup Organization, Inc., Princeton, New Jersey.
3. National Teacher Examination (N.T.E.), by Educational Testing Service, Princeton, New Jersey.
4. Sizer, Theodore R., Chairperson, Department of Education, Brown University, Profidence, R.I.
5. Boyer, Ernest L., President, Carnegie Foundation for the Advancement of Teaching, Princeton, New Jersey; Former U.S. Secretary of Education under Carter administration.

Chapter 8: The Rising Mediocrity

1. Solokovits, Judy, Head, Los Angeles Teachers Union, Los Angeles, California.
2. Boyer, Ernest L., President, Carnegie Foundation for the Advancement of Teaching, Princeton, New Jersey; Former U.S. Secretary of Education under Carter administration.
3. Ravitch, Dr. Diane, Professor of Education, Teachers College, Columbia University, New York, N.Y.

PART III: THE PERILOUS DECADE: PUBLIC FAITH

Chapter 9: Desertion by the Middle Class

1. Goodlad, Dr. John, Professor (Former Dean) of Education, University of California, Los Angeles, CA.

2. National Commission on Excellence on Education. *A Nation at Risk: The Imperative for Education Reform,* Washington, D.C., 1983.

3. Sizer, Theodore R., Chairperson, Department of Education, Brown University, Providence, R.I.

Chapter 10: Decreased Financial Support

1. American Association of Fund Raising Council, Inc., New York, N.Y., annual report, 1983.

2. Reagan, Ronald, President of the United States. "Excellence and Opportunity: A Program of Support for American Education," Kansas City, Missouri, 1984.

3. Boyer, Ernest L., President, Carnegie Foundation for the Advancement of Teaching, Princeton, New Jersey; Former U.S. Secretary of Education under Carter administration.

4. Bell, Terrell, Former U.S. Secretary of Education under Reagan administration.

5. Goodlad, Dr. John, Professor (Former Dean) of Education, University of California, Los Angeles, CA.

6. Stovall, Ashton, a Founder of the Reform Movement, Kansas schools.

Chapter 11: Curriculum Concensus

1. Ravitch, Dr. Diane, Professor of Education, Teachers College, Columbia University, New Yor, N.Y.

2. Institute for Educational Leadership, *Early Alert: The Impact of Federal Education Cutbacks on the States,* Washington, D.C. 1982.

PART IV: THE PERILOUS DECADE: THE FINAL PERIL

1. Goodlad, Dr. John, (Former Dean) of Education, University of California, Los Angeles, California.

2. Ravitch, Dr. Diane, Professor of Education, Teachers College, Columbia University, New York, N.Y.

3. Boyer, Ernest L., President, Carnegie Foundation for the Advancement of Teaching, Princeton, New Jersey; Former U.S. Secretary of Education under Carter administration.

4. Sizer, Theodore R. Chairperson, Department of Education, Brown University, Profidence, R.I.

SOURCE NOTES

PART V: THE PERILOUS DECADE: CANDLES IN THE DARKNESS

1. Perot, H. Ross, Head of Commission to Improve the Public Education System, Texas.
2. Hollander, T. Edward, Chancellor of Higher Education, Trenton, New Jersey.
3. Duke, Dr. Robert E., *A Report on Successful and Innovative Programs in New England Schools*, Quincy, Massachusetts, 1985.
4. The Forum of Educational Organization Leaders, pub. November 1983.
5. National Education Association, Washington, D.C.
6. American Federation of teachers, Washington, D.C.
7. Business and Higher Education Forum, *America's Competitive Challenge: The Need for a National Response*, Washington, D.C., 1983.
8. Education Commission of The States, *A Summary of Major Reports on Education*, Denver, Colorado, 1983.
9. Task Force on Education for Economic Growth, Action for Excellence: *A Comprehensive Plan to Improve Our Nation's Schools*, Education Commission of The States, Denver, Colorado, 1983.
10. Twentieth Century Fund Report of the Twentieth Century Fund Task Force on Federal Elementary and Secondary Education Policy, New York, N.Y., 1983.

APPENDIXES: INNOVATIVE IDEAS AND PROGRAMS

Appendix A: Assisting Latchkey Children

1. Seligson, Michelle, Director, School-Age Child Care, project of Wellesley College, Wellesley, Mass.
2. Project Phone-A-Friend, est. by American Association of University Women, Pennsylvania State University Chapter, University Park, PA.
3. Friedman, Dana, "Day Care in America," *Reader's Digest*, June 1985.
4. Senate Bill S. 2565, U.S. Congress, Washington, D.C., October 1984.
5. High Scope Educational Research Foundation, Ypsilanti, Mich.

Appendix B: Aiding Disadvantaged Pupils

1. High Scope Educational Research Foundation, Ypsilanti, Mich.
2. Hardy, Dorcas, Assistant Secretary, U.S. Department of Health and Human Services, Washington, D.C.

3. S.A.D.I.E. Program, Palm Beach County Schools, Palm Beach, Fla.

4. Geselle, Arnold, Child Psychiatrist, Former Director of the Clinic of Child Development, School of Medicine, Yale University, New Haven, Connecticut; author of *Infant and Child in the Culture Today*.

5. Duke, Dr. Robert E., *A Report on Successful and Innovative Programs in New England Schools*, Quincy, Massachusetts, 1985.

Appendix C: Dealing With Older Students

1. Boyer, Ernest, "High School: A Report on Secondary Education in America," Carnegie Foundation for the Advancement of Teaching, Princeton, New Jersey, 1983.

2. Duke, Dr. Robert E., *A Report on Successful and Innovative Programs in New England Schools*, Quincy, Massachusetts, 1982.

3. "Walkabout" Program, Jefferson County Open High School, Evergreen, Colorado.

4. "Walkabout" Program, Yorktown School, Yorktown, New York.

5. New Garden Friends School, Greensboro, N. Carolina.

6. Winter Park High School, Winter Park, Fla.

7. Levin, Henry, Glass, Gene, and Meister, Gail, Institute for Research on Educational Finance and Governance, Stanford University, Stanford, Ca.

8. Leon D. Brandeis School, New York, N.Y.

9. Forsyth-Satellite Academy, New York, N.Y.

10. Cooperative Federation for Educational experience (C.O.F.F.E.E.), Oxford, Mass.

11. Futrell, Mary Hatwood, President, National Education Association, Washington, D.C.

12. How, Harold II, Harvard Graduate School of Education, Harvard University, Cambridge, Mass.; Former U.S. Commissioner of Education.

13. Peter Stuyvesant High School, New York, N.Y.

14. Brooklyn Technical High School, New York, N.Y.

15. School of the Performing Arts, New York, N.Y.

16. Aviation High School, New York, N.Y.

17. Bronx High School of Science, New York, N.Y.

18. Edward R. Murrow High School, New York, N.Y.

19. John Ericsson Junior High School, New York, N.Y.

20. LeyVa Junior High School, San Jose, CA.

21. Adler, Mortimer J., *Paideia Problems and Possibilities*, Institute for Philosophical Research, 1983.

Appendix D: Restoring Teacher Confidence and Competence

1. Comprehensive Education Reform Act, state legislature, Nashville, Tennessee, 1984.

SOURCE NOTES

2. Sub. H.B. 1246, U.S. Congress, Washington, D.C., 1984.

3. "The NEA Plan For School Reform," a report adopted by the 1985 representative assembly of the National Education Association, Washington, D.C.

4. PACE (Polling Attitudes of the Community on Education), Phi Delta Kappa, Blooomington, IN.

5. Shanker, Albert, President and Executive Director, American Federation of Teachers, Washington, D.C.

6. Harvard Principal Center, Harvard University, Cambridge, Mass.

7. PROTEACH Program, College of Education, University of Florida, Miami, Fla.

8. American Association of Colleges for Teacher Education (AACTE), Bicentennial report, "Educating a Profession," Washington, D.C., 1976.

9. School of Education, Oregon State University/West Oregon State College (OSU/WOSC) "Warranty Assurance Program," Corvallis, Oregon.

10. Greenville Public School System Recertification Program, Greenville, S. Carolina.

11. Yale-New Haven Teachers Institute, Yale University, New Haven, Conn.

12. Feistritzer, Emily C., *The Condition of Teaching: A State by State Analysis,* Carnegie Foundation, Princeton, New Jersey, 1983.

13. Musconomet Regional School District, Topsfield, Mass.

14. "Teacher Recognition Task Force," Council Bluffs, Iowa.

15. Columbia University, New York, N.Y.

16. New York University, New York, N.Y.

17. National PTA (National Congress of Parents and Teachers Association), Chicago, IL.

18. Dalton Public School System, Dalton, Ca.

19. McKenna, Charles, Superintendent, Ledue Public School System, Ledue, Mo.

20. Genck, Frederic, School Board President, Lake Forest, Ill.

21. Alexander, Bruce, School Board President, Round Valley, CA.

22. National Teacher Examination (N.T.E.) by Educational Testing Service, Princeton, New Jersey.

Appendix E: Regaining Public Support

1. Ritchie, Miller, Former President, Hartwick College, Oneonta, N.Y.

2. Pawlas, George E., Principal, Leaphart Elementary School, Columbia, S. Carolian.

3. Duke, Dr. Robert E., *A Report on Successful and Innovative Programs in New England Schools,* Quincy, Massachusetts, 1985.

4. Public Policy Analysis Service poll, Public Policy Analysis, Inc., Washington, D.C., Fall 1983.

5. Gallup Polls, Gallup Organization, Inc., Princeton, New Jersey, 1983, 1984.

6. Teeter, Robert M. and Hart Peter, public opinion researchers.

7. National Conference of State Legislatures, Denver, Colorado, October 1983.

8. *Newsweek* Poll, February 27, 1984, p. 44.